Bloom's BioCritiques

Dante Alighieri
Maya Angelou
Jane Austen
Jorge Luis Borges
The Brontë Sisters
Gwendolyn Brooks
Lord Byron
Miguel de Cervantes
Geoffrey Chaucer
Anton Chekhov
Joseph Conrad
Stephen Crane
Charles Dickens
Emily Dickinson
Fyodor Dostoevsky
William Faulkner
F. Scott Fitzgerald
Robert Frost
Ernest Hemingway
Langston Hughes
Zora Neale Hurston
Franz Kafka
Stephen King
Arthur Miller
John Milton
Toni Morrison
Edgar Allan Poe
J.D. Salinger
William Shakespeare
John Steinbeck
Henry David Thoreau
Mark Twain
Alice Walker
Eudora Welty
Walt Whitman
Tennessee Williams
Virginia Woolf

Bloom's BioCritiques

VIRGINIA WOOLF

Edited and with an introduction by
Harold Bloom
Sterling Professor of the Humanities
Yale University

CHELSEA HOUSE
PUBLISHERS
A Haights Cross Communications Company
Philadelphia

A Haights Cross Communications Company

http://www.chelseahouse.com

Contributing editor: Neil Heims
Cover design by Keith Trego
Cover: © Hulton | Archive by Getty Images, Inc.
Layout by EJB Publishing Services

Library of Congress Cataloging-in-Publication Data

Virginia Woolf / Harold Bloom, editor.
     p. cm. — (Bloom's biocritiques)
  Includes bibliographical references and index.
  ISBN 0-7910-7873-6 (alk. paper)
  1. Woolf, Virginia, 1882-1941—Criticism and interpretation. 2. Women and
literature—England—History—20th century. I. Bloom, Harold. II. Series.
  PR6045.O72Z8918 2004
  823'.912—dc22
                                2004013705

CONTENTS

USER'S GUIDE

These volumes are designed to introduce the reader to the life and work of the world's literary masters. Each volume begins with Harold Bloom's essay "The Work in the Writer" and a volume-specific introduction also written by Professor Bloom. Following these unique introductions is an engaging biography that discusses the major life events and important literary accomplishments of the author under consideration.

Furthermore, each volume includes an original critique that not only traces the themes, symbols, and ideas apparent in the author's works, but strives to put those works into a cultural and historical perspective. In addition to the original critique is a brief selection of significant critical essays previously published on the author and his or her works followed by a concise and informative chronology of the writer's life. Finally, each volume concludes with a bibliography of the writer's works, a list of additional readings, and an index of important themes and ideas.

HAROLD BLOOM

The Work in the Writer

Literary biography found its masterpiece in James Boswell's *Life of Samuel Johnson*. Boswell, when he treated Johnson's writings, implicitly commented upon Johnson as found in his work, even as in the great critic's life. Modern instances of literary biography, such as Richard Ellmann's lives of W.B. Yeats, James Joyce, and Oscar Wilde, essentially follow in Boswell's pattern.

That the writer somehow is in the work, we need not doubt, though with William Shakespeare, writer-of-writers, we almost always need to rely upon pure surmise. The exquisite rancidities of the Problem Plays or Dark Comedies seem to express an extraordinary estrangement of Shakespeare from himself. When we read or attend *Troilus and Cressida* and *Measure for Measure*, we may be startled by particular speeches of Ulysses in the first play, or of Vincentio in the second. These speeches, of Ulysses upon hierarchy or upon time, or of Duke Vincentio upon death, are too strong either for their contexts or for the characters of their speakers. The same phenomenon occurs with Parolles, the military impostor of *All's Well That Ends Well*. Utterly disgraced, he nevertheless affirms: "Simply the thing I am / Shall make me live."

In Shakespeare, more even than in his peers, Dante and Cervantes, meaning always starts itself again through excess or overflow. The strongest of Shakespeare's creatures—Falstaff, Hamlet, Iago, Lear, Cleopatra—have an exuberance that is fiercer than their plays can contain. If Ben Jonson was at all correct in his complaint that "Shakespeare wanted art," it could have been only in a sense that he may not have intended. Where do the personalities of Falstaff or Hamlet touch a limit? What was it in Shakespeare that made *Hamlet* and the two parts of *Henry IV* into "plays unlimited"? Neither Falstaff nor Hamlet will be stopped: their wit, their beautiful, laughing speech, their intensity of being—all these are virtually infinite.

In what ways do Falstaff and Hamlet manifest the writer in the work? Evidently, we can never know, or know enough to answer with any authority. But what would happen if we reversed the question, and asked: How did the work form the writer, Shakespeare?

Of Shakespeare's inwardness, his biography tells us nothing. And yet, to an astonishing extent, Shakespeare created our inwardness. At the least, we can speculate that Shakespeare so lived his life as to conceal the depths of his nature, particularly as he rather prematurely aged. We do not have Shakespeare on Shakespeare, as any good reader of the Sonnets comes to realize: they do not constitute a key that unlocks his heart. No sequence of sonnets could be less confessional or more powerfully detached from the poet's self.

The German poet and universal genius, Goethe, affords a superb contrast to Shakespeare. Of Goethe's life, we know more than everything; I wonder sometimes if we know as much about Napoleon or Freud or any other human being who ever has lived, as we know about Goethe. Everywhere, we can find Goethe in his work, so much so that Goethe seems to crowd the writing out, just as Byron and Oscar Wilde seem to usurp their own literary accomplishments. Goethe, cunning beyond measure, nevertheless invested a rival exuberance in his greatest works that could match his personal charisma. The sublime out-rageousness of the Second Part of *Faust*, or of the greater lyric and meditative poems, forms a Counter-Sublime to Goethe's own daemonic intensity.

Goethe was fascinated by the daemonic in himself; we can doubt that Shakespeare had any such interests. Evidently, Shakespeare abandoned his acting career just before he composed *Measure for Measure* and *Othello*. I surmise that the egregious interventions by Vincentio and Iago displace the actor's energies into a new kind of mischief-making, a fresh opening to a subtler playwriting-within-the-play.

But what had opened Shakespeare to this new awareness? The answer is the work in the writer, *Hamlet* in Shakespeare. One can go further: it was not so much the play, *Hamlet*, as the character Hamlet, who changed Shakespeare's art forever.

Hamlet's personality is so large and varied that it rivals Goethe's own. Ironically Goethe's Faust, his Hamlet, has no personality at all, and is as colorless as Shakespeare himself seems to have chosen to be. Yet nothing could be more colorful than the Second Part of *Faust*, which is peopled by an astonishing array of monsters, grotesque devils and classical ghosts.

A contrast between Shakespeare and Goethe demonstrates that in each—but in very different ways—we can better find the work in the person, than we can discover that banal entity, the person in the work. Goethe to many of his contemporaries seemed to be a mortal god. Shakespeare, so far as we know, seemed an affable, rather ordinary fellow, who aged early and became somewhat withdrawn. Yet Faust, though Mephistopheles battles for his soul, is hardly worth the trouble unless you take him as an idea and not as a person. Hamlet is nearly every-idea-in-one, but he is precisely a personality and a person.

Would Hamlet be so astonishingly persuasive if his father's ghost did not haunt him? Falstaff is more alive than Prince Hal, who says that the devil haunts him in the shape of an old fat man. Three years before composing the final *Hamlet*, Shakespeare invented Falstaff, who then never ceased to haunt his creator. Falstaff and Hamlet may be said to best represent the work in the writer, because their influence upon Shakespeare was prodigious. W.H. Auden accurately observed that Falstaff possesses infinite energy: never tired, never bored, and absolutely both witty and happy until Hal's rejection destroys him. Hamlet too has infinite energy, but in him it is more curse than blessing.

Falstaff and Hamlet can be said to occupy the roles in Shakespeare's invented world that Sancho Panza and Don Quixote possess in Cervantes's. Shakespeare's plays from 1610 on (starting with *Twelfth Night*) are thus analogous to the Second Part of Cervantes's epic novel. Sancho and the Don overtly jostle Cervantes for authorship in the Second Part, even as Cervantes battles against the impostor who has pirated a continuation of his work. As a dramatist, Shakespeare manifests the work in the writer more indirectly. Falstaff's prose genius is revived in the scapegoating of Malvolio by Maria and Sir Toby Belch, while Falstaff's darker insights are developed by Feste's melancholic wit. Hamlet's intellectual resourcefulness, already deadly, becomes poisonous in Iago and in Edmund. Yet we have not crossed into the deeper abysses of the work in the writer in later Shakespeare.

No fictive character, before or since, is Falstaff's equal in self-trust. Sir John, whose delight in himself is contagious, has total confidence both in his self-awareness and in the resources of his language. Hamlet, whose self is as strong, and whose language is as copious, nevertheless distrusts both the self and language. Later Shakespeare is, as it were, much under the influence both of Falstaff and of Hamlet, but they tug him in opposite directions. Shakespeare's own copiousness of language is well-nigh incredible: a vocabulary in excess of twenty-one thousand words, almost eighteen hundred of which he coined himself. And of his word-hoard, nearly half are used only once each, as though the perfect setting for each had been found, and need not be repeated. Love for language and faith in language are Falstaffian attributes. Hamlet will darken both that love and that faith in Shakespeare, and perhaps the Sonnets can best be read as Falstaff and Hamlet counterpointing against one another.

Can we surmise how aware Shakespeare was of Falstaff and Hamlet, once they had played themselves into existence? *Henry IV, Part I* appeared in six quarto editions during Shakespeare's lifetime; *Hamlet* possibly had four. Falstaff and Hamlet were played again and again at the Globe, but Shakespeare knew also that they were being read, and he must have had contact with some of those readers. What would it have been like to discuss Falstaff or Hamlet with one of their early readers (presumably also part of their audience at the Globe), if you were the creator of such demiurges? The question would seem nonsensical to most Shakespeare scholars, but then these days they tend to be either ideologues or moldy figs. How can we recover the uncanniness of Falstaff and of Hamlet, when they now have become so familiar?

A writer's influence upon himself is an unexplored problem in criticism, but such an influence is never free from anxieties. The biocritical problem (which this series attempts to explore) can be divided into two areas, difficult to disengage fully. Accomplished works affect the author's life, and also affect her subsequent writings. It is simpler for me to surmise the effect of *Mrs. Dalloway* and *To the Lighthouse* upon Woolf's late *Between the Acts*, than it is to relate Clarissa Dalloway's suicide and Lily Briscoe's capable endurance in art to the tragic death and complex life of Virginia Woolf.

There are writers whose lives were so vivid that they seem sometimes to obscure the literary achievement: Byron, Wilde, Malraux, Hemingway. But most major Western writers do not live that exuberantly, and the greatest of all, Shakespeare, sometimes appears to have adopted the personal mask of colorlessness. And yet there are heroes of literature who struggled titanically with their own eras—Tolstoy, Milton, Victor Hugo—who nevertheless matter more for their works than their lives.

There are great figures—Emily Dickinson, Wallace Stevens, Willa Cather—who seem to have had so little of the full intensity of life when compared to the vitality of their work, that we might almost speak of the work in the work, rather than even of the work in a person. Emily Brontë might well be the extreme instance of such a visionary, surpassing William Blake in that one regard.

I conclude this general introduction to a series of literary bio-critiques by stating a tentative formula or principle for gauging the many ways in which the work influences the person and her subsequent, later work. Our influence upon ourselves is always related to the Shakespearean invention of self-overhearing, which I have written about in several other contexts. Life, as well as poetry and prose, is overheard rather than simply heard. The writer listens to herself as though she were somebody else, and the will to change begins to operate. The forces that live in us include the prior work we have done, and the dreams and waking visions that evade our dismissals.

HAROLD BLOOM

Introduction

Virginia Woolf was one of the most original novelists of the century now passed. Her life was a long, heroic struggle against madness. Her first breakdown was precipitated, at thirteen, by the death of her mother. The death of her father, Leslie Stephen, when she was twenty-two, stimulated a second breakdown and an attempted suicide. A third crisis lasted for three years, from thirty to thirty-three. Finally, under the terrible stress of German air bombardment, Woolf drowned herself at the age of fifty-nine.

Woolf's major novels, by common consent, are *Mrs. Dalloway* (1925) and *To the Lighthouse* (1927). *Orlando* (1928) remains popular, but is a secondary work. Her later novels are all extraordinary work, and clearly will survive: *The Waves* (1931), *The Years* (1937), and a final masterpiece, *Between the Acts* (1941). Formally speaking, Woolf's finest novel is *To the Lighthouse*, which is a miraculous concentration of her varied gifts.

Woolf has become the high priestess of feminist literary criticism, since she insists that the creative power of women "differs greatly from the creative power of man." Iris Murdoch refreshingly disagreed: "I think there's human experience; and I don't think a woman's mind differs essentially from a man's." There are major *male* novelists—Samuel Richardson, Tolstoy, Henry James—who have explored female consciousness perhaps more fully than did Jane Austen and Virginia Woolf. One can add Marcel Proust and James Joyce, whose depictions of inwardness are equally strong, whether women or men are being portrayed.

Woolf sought her precursors in Jane Austen and Emily Brontë, but in temperament and artistic stance she scarcely resembles either. The true precursor, as Perry Meisel has shown, was Walter Pater, whose sensibility hovers everywhere in Woolf. Her profound aestheticism is precisely Paterian: perception and sensation are what matter most as we face the universe of death. Woolf's relation to Pater is analogous to Proust's to Ruskin. Pater's *Imaginary Portraits* already are Woolfian, as Ruskin's *Praeterita* is Proustian.

Feminist critics have not confronted the difficulties of reconciling Woolf's aestheticism with their ideological means test for literature. Except for her aestheticism, the author of *Mrs. Dalloway* and *To the Lighthouse* would be wholly nihilistic, which is true also of Pater, Ruskin, and Proust. Woolf teaches perception, and not politics. Her "androgyny" is not a pragmatic cause, but a fusion of perception and sensation with her acceptance of death and meaninglessness, apart from the flow of momentary meanings that art can suggest.

Woolf's ambivalence towards James Joyce betrays the anxiety of a common ancestry in Paterian solipsism, with its reliance upon epiphanies or privileged moments. Woolf's father, the empiricist Leslie Stephen, loathed Pater and, as Mr. Ramsay in *To the Lighthouse*, utters a rugged motto: "The very stone one kicks with one's boot will outlast Shakespeare."

Clarissa Dalloway, staring at herself in the mirror, saves herself from the madness that destroys Septimus, her daemon or soul's brother, by a Paterian vision of the self, crystal and diamond. As readers, we accept the reality of Mrs. Dalloway's self because of her marvelously articulated memories, which Woolf had the cunning to invent so as to give her character some distancing from Woolf herself:

> No, Lytton does not like Mrs. Dalloway, &, what is odd, I like him all the better for saying so, & don't much mind. What he says is that there is a discordancy between the ornament (extremely beautiful) & what happens (rather ordinary—or unimportant). This is caused he thinks by some discrepancy in Clarissa herself; he thinks remarkably, with myself. So that I think as a whole, the book does not ring solid; yet, he says, it is a whole; & he says sometimes the writing is of extreme beauty. What can one call it but genius? he said! Coming when, one never can tell. Fuller of genius,

he said, than anything I had done. Perhaps, he said, you have not yet mastered your method. You should take something wilder & more fantastic, a frame work that admits of anything, like Tristram Shandy. But then I should lose touch with emotions, I said. Yes, he agreed, there must be reality for you to start from. Heaven knows how you're to do it. But he thought me at the beginning, not at the end. And he said the C.R. {The Common Reader} was divine, a classic; Mrs. D. being, I fear, a flawed stone. This is very personal, he said & old fashioned perhaps; yet I think there is some truth in it. For I remember the night at Rodmell when I decided to give it up, because I found Clarissa in some way tinselly. Then I invented her memories. But I think some distaste for her persisted. Yet, again, that was true to my feelings for Kitty {Maxse}, & one must dislike people in art without its mattering, unless indeed it is true that certain characters detract from the importance of what happens to them.

"A flawed stone" or a diamond: which is the accurate judgment upon Clarissa Dalloway? If she is a diamond, then it is only because of the extraordinary doubling between her and Septimus Smith, who will never meet one another. They share a single consciousness, precariously on the edge of life. Septimus dies Clarissa's death for her:

> She had once thrown a shilling into the Serpentine, never anything more. But he had flung it away. They went on living (she would have to go back; the rooms were still crowded; people kept on coming). They (all day she had been thinking of Bourton, of Peter, of Sally), they would grow old. A thing there was that mattered; a thing, wreathed about with chatter, defaced, obscured in her own life, let drop every day in corruption, lies, chatter. This he had preserved. Death was defiance. Death was an attempt to communicate; people feeling the impossibility of reaching the centre which, mystically, evaded them; closeness drew apart; rapture faded, one was alone. There was an embrace in death.

Suicide is a communication, since the mystical center otherwise evades us. Direct experience, in life or in literature, recedes from us the more eagerly we seek for it. Woolf's novels forsake the naturalism that alienated her in James Joyce, in favor—not of symbolism—but of Pater's impressionism.

CAMILLE-YVETTE WELSH

Biography of Virginia Woolf

She might have become a glorified *diseuse*, who frittered away her broader effects by mischievousness, and she did give that impression to some who met her in the flesh; there were moments when she could scarcely see the busts for the moustaches she pencilled on them, and when the bust was a modern one, whether of a gentleman in a top hat or a youth on a pylon, it had no chance of remaining sublime. But in her writing, even in her light writing, central control entered. She was master of her complicated equipment, and though most of us like to write sometimes seriously and sometimes in fun, few of us can so manage the two impulses that they speed each other up, as hers did.
—E.M. Forster, from *Virginia Woolf* (The Rede Lecture) (1942)

INTRODUCTION

Over the years the popular media has engaged in an ad campaign selling madness as a select part of literary genius. Whether the movie is *Sylvia* or *The Hours*, some of literature's most famous women have been subject to public scrutiny and conjecture regarding their suicides, the impetus for such a drastic action, and the relation of madness to writing (of course, in many ways, they are only following in the footsteps of some literary criticism). Clearly, for Woolf, the answers remain much more complex than any movie can ever articulate. Some suggest that Woolf's suicide resulted from an old madness which again resurfaced, and that the terrified Woolf chose to take her own life rather than subject herself to the tortures of her former experience with mental illness. Others claim that it was born of a nervous disposition, an inability to cope with the bombings and terror England was subject to during World War II. Still others suggest that it was her unwillingness to burden her husband with the madness that she felt creeping up on her. Whatever the cause, visions of Woolf must contend with those created by Hollywood, of a tall, gaunt woman carefully placing notes on the mantel, one for her husband and one for her sister, then putting on her coat and hat and walking out the door, knowing that she leaves behind a devastated husband and grief-stricken sister, and knowing that ahead of her lies a deep, fast-running river, and an escape from the slow suffocation of breakdown. She places heavy rocks in the pockets of her coat, ensuring that this time, she will stay at the bottom of the river and not resurface before her lungs fill with water. When she finally fully gives in to the movement of the river, her hat floats slowly away from her head, downstream. Both the movie *The Hours* and the critics agree that the moment was quiet and not one of great melodrama; indeed the rhythms match those of Woolf's greatest novels. She is deliberate, calm, and inevitable. Her character, one she spent her life creating, has reached what could be the only end to her story, and this time the greatest character she has ever created would pass from the world into a watery grave, and the rhythm and method would match the watery movement of her stories.

Virginia Woolf is known for many things: her central membership in the Bloomsbury Group, her feminist tracts, her troubled and redeeming marriage, her lesbian tendencies, her articulate essays, her vibrant conversation, her heritage, her beauty, her part in the Hogarth Press, her radical narrative forms, and her contribution to modernism. As a child, death was ever-present in her world. She suffered the loss of her mother, her aunt, her half-sister, her father, her cousin, and many family friends while still in young adulthood. Virginia began to write early, as a mode of coping with the pain of loss. She reconciled life through the revisionary process of writing. She could recapture what she had lost, make it beautiful, control it, and convince herself that she was real and worthwhile, all through her writing.

... [T]hough I still have the peculiarity that I receive these sudden shocks, they are now always welcome; after the first surprise, I always feel instantly that they are particularly valuable. And so I go on to suppose that the shock-receiving capacity is what makes me a writer. I hazard the explanation that a shock is at once in my case followed by the desire to explain it. I feel that I have had a blow; but it is not, as I thought as a child, simply a blow from an enemy hidden behind the cotton wool of daily life; it is or will become a revelation of some order; it is a token of some real thing behind appearances; and I make it real by putting it into words. It is only by putting it into words that I make it whole; this wholeness means that it has lost its power to hurt me; it gives me, perhaps because by doing so I take away the pain, a great delight to put the severed pieces together. Perhaps this is the greatest pleasure known to me (Woolf, 72).

PARENTAL BURDEN

It may well be said that Virginia Woolf entered directly into the literary world via her father, Leslie Stephen, editor of *The Dictionary of National Biography* and *The Cornhill Magazine*, and author of *Hours in a Library, Mausoleum Book, History of English Thought in the Eighteenth Century*, and *The Playground of Europe*, as well as many articles on his literary friends, religion, and other critical reviews. Leslie Stephen was the fourth of five children, and as a boy he was unnaturally sensitive, desperate for his mother's approval and sympathy. She writes of her young son that he was the "most independent-spirited little fellow, very bold and very persevering ... and seems to have no fear at all when he is trying to do anything ... He is rather violent in his temper, and, if displeased, will cry out most loudly" (Leaska, 20). This obsessive need for affirmation and adoration continued throughout his life, making his household one ever full of turbulence and high emotion; it was an obsessive behavior that his daughter would mirror. At school, Stephen was often teased and bullied, only relieved by the intervention of his elder brother, James Fitzjames, a burly, independent boy who protected his skinny, ungainly brother. While Leslie did not excel in social engagements, he proved to be a more than adequate student as a day-boy at Eton. He eventually left for Cambridge, where he studied at Trinity Hall, and sick of his own seeming frailty, he gathered his formidable will and endeavored to become an athlete, subsequently joining the crew team and later coaching it. After his first year, he received a scholarship, and by the end of his fourth year, he was offered a fellowship, one which necessitated the taking of Holy Orders. In 1855, at the age of twenty-three, he took the Orders and became an ordained deacon, then in 1856, a junior tutor. But the position of religious lackey did not sit well with the independent-minded Stephen, who was becoming increasingly dissatisfied with his life as a clergyman, largely due to his reading of "Mill, Comte, Hobbes and the British empiricists" (Leaska, 23). Unfortunately, such disillusionment also meant the loss of his financially and personally comfortable place at the University. Stephen chose to follow his principles in his own admirable and rigid way. He resigned the University based on his objection to religion and became a professional journalist, as his daughter later would. He wrote for *The Saturday Review*, *The Pall Mall Gazette*, and *The Cornhill Magazine*, among others, accumulating clips and a reputation as a man of unerring taste and broad reference, a true Victorian man of letters (Leaska, 24). At the end of the 19th century, his biographer, Noel Annan, wrote that no one "could match both the enormous range of his reading and the intellectual power under perfect control which expressed itself in a fluent, sinewy style" (Leaska, 28).

At thirty-four, terrified of being a bachelor all of his life, Stephen decided to marry William Thackeray's daughter Harriet Marian (Minny), a not-terribly-bright but very supportive young woman; however, after the birth of a mentally deficient daughter, Laura, in December 1870, the union was short-lived, ending with the death of Minny after eight years of marriage. Stephen was devastated. He was afraid of being left alone, with no one to take care of him. Minny was survived by a sister, Annie, a writer, who took over the household, but her nature had always clashed with his, whether it be their wrangling over the affections of the dead sister, the behavior of Minny's surviving daughter, or the illicit love affair between Annie and her godson, seventeen years her junior. Stephen happened upon the two kissing in the drawing room one day and was so offended that he ordered Annie to either marry the boy or get out of the house. She left. His own sister stepped in briefly, but within a very few days, Stephen turned to the widow next door, a Mrs. Julia Duckworth to become his helpmate.

Julia Prinsep Jackson (Duckworth Stephen) was born in February 1846 in India. In 1848, she returned to England, and grew up often visiting the family of her mother's sister at Little Holland House, a sort of refuge for artists and writers. Julia was a stunningly beautiful woman, having already received two proposals of marriage before, as Virginia Woolf would later put it, "she was scarcely out of the nursery" (Leaska, 27). She posed for many artists, Edward Burne-Jones, G.F. Watts, Carlo Marochetti and her aunt Julia Cameron among them (Leaska, 27). The effect of this beauty caused Julia Jackson to turn to many things, such as tending to the sick, and perfecting the social order; if she was to be remembered, it would be not only for her beauty but for her soul as well. From the sick, she derived the feeling of being needed, and again, the emphasis is being needed not for aesthetic value but for the pragmatics of easing affliction. When Julia was ten, her mother began to feel the affliction of rheumatism; she needed her youngest daughter to tend her. Julia threw herself into the task, happy to be needed, unconsciously aware of the power it gave one. She tended her mother for the next ten years, accepting the occasional travel break to visit her sisters. At eighteen, while visiting in Venice, she met her sister's friend, the handsome Herbert Duckworth whom she later married and with whom she had three children: George (1868), Stella (1869), and Gerald (1870). Virginia remembers her mother claiming of the marriage, that in it, she was "as happy as anyone can be" (Leaska, 40).

During her married life, Julia had three children within the first four years of her marriage, then her husband died suddenly and Julia found herself widowed and depressed. Virginia wrote of his death that "like all very handsome men who die tragically, he left not so much a character behind him as a legend" (Leaska, 40–1). Virginia believed her mother to have always been pining for Duckworth, a true love that Leslie Stephen was never able to measure up to. His ghost even walks through the pages of *To the Lighthouse*; Duckworth is the presence in the garden, the shadow in the distance to which Mrs. Ramsey is always looking (Leaska, 42–43).

After the death of her husband, she moved and found that her old friend Minny Thackeray was living next door with her child, Laura, and her husband, Leslie Stephen, a man whose work Julia found sympathetic, particularly his treatises on agnosticism. After Minny's death, and two ill-suited family members' attempts at keeping house for Leslie, Julia took over the running of the Stephen household, and after a long courtship of letters and visits, she agreed to marry the ever-needy Stephen.

Within the first four years of marriage, Julia bore four children: Vanessa in 1879, Julian Thoby, 1880, Adrian, 1883, and Adeline Virginia Stephen, born on January 25, 1882. She provided the constant sympathy and affirmation Stephen sought and managed his household to Victorian perfection. Part of her duty was later explained to Vanessa, who Stephen was grooming to take the place of his deceased wife and stepdaughter: "When he was sad, he explained, she should be sad; when he was angry ... she should weep." (Woolf, *Moments of Being* 50)Julia's burden in her marriage to Stephen was great; she cared for eight children, one of whom needed extra care due to her mental instability; she cared for the sick, the dying, and the infirm, and for her extended family; she wrote a treatise on nursing; she took care of Stephen's constant and insistent bids for sympathy, and she acted as the perfect Victorian hostess. When she died in 1895, it was as much from exhaustion as rheumatism, and her work in the sickroom made death a constant presence in her children's lives, with aunts, uncles, cousins and grandparents passing away around them. Still, it would be unfair to posit Julia as a victim. She chose Stephen in large part for his neediness. She had known love, and felt that she would never have it again. She was aging; her personality was, in its own way, as needy as his. She longed for a position of power such as that of caretaker. She also felt a Victorian dislike for women of political power; instead, she chose to wield her power in the social arena by making guests and patients alike feel comfortable with and beholden to her.

Life for Virginia followed the routine of many other children during her early years. The children lived and played in the nursery until the boys were old enough for school, which they then attended, leaving behind their two sisters to the tutelage of their parents and later a collection of governesses. Julia pored over their books with them at the long dining room table, and Stephen tried to bully them into learning math. Virginia showed an early aptitude for languages, history, and literature, encouraging her father to view her as his particular protégé. All of the children were fascinated by the outdoors, following in the footsteps of their hill-walking father; they took long walks along the beaches in Cornwall, caught butterflies and moths with their nets, waded in the ocean, played with and studied books (Virginia was in charge of researching the actual names of the bugs they caught), and playing cricket and bowls (Virginia was named by her siblings "the demon bowler"). Their home in Hyde Park Gate was in the Kensington section of London, which retained the feel of a small upper-middle-class community full of social taboos and gossip, but also was fairly safe for the jaunt in the park or children playing outside. The Stephens knew most of their neighbors and were felt to be proprietary members of the community. It was a place that the wild Stephen siblings would inevitably outgrow and escape after the death of their parents.

In marriage, Virginia's parents were in a near-constant battle to outworry each other, to be more pathetic or more powerful by turns. Stephen claimed constant illness, nervousness from working on *The Dictionary of Literary Biography*, from writing lectures to be given at Trinity College, Cambridge, from writing the lives of dead literary friends, and from worry about money and health. He had terrible headaches, nightmares, and fits. He needed Julia to talk him to sleep and convince him that his was not a wasted life. Julia responded by claiming that it hurt her how much he loved her, that she feared always hurting him because she was not worthy of his love, and she too suffered from over-extending herself. When Virginia entered into close relationships in her life, it was with this pattern in mind, making many of her closest engagements distrustful, tense, codependent, passive-aggressive, and competitive.

VICTORIAN CHILDHOOD

The two nurseries at the top of the house in Hyde Park Gate were tightly knit places where Virginia loved most fiercely her brother Thoby and her sister, Vanessa. Adrian remained a distant third in her affections all of her life, and the Duckworth children were more distant still. Virginia vied with Vanessa throughout childhood for the affection of Thoby, envying the time that they had together prior to her birth. As a result, the threesome was often at odds, though never dull. Vanessa Bell remembers in "Notes on Virginia's Childhood" roaming around Kensington Gardens and finding the body of a black dog; Virginia's sarcasm; her sister, labeling her "The Saint," "quickly reducing [Vanessa] to the misery of sarcasm from the grown-ups as well as the nursery world," (Stape, 3) and telling stories after bedtime of the family next door by the name of Dilke, whom they "mocked for not being able to pronounce the letter R" (Stape, 5). She also recalls a bout of whooping cough, which she suggests was a particular turning point for Virginia, believing that as the others recovered from 'little skeletons' back to children, that Virginia simply moved "into some new layer of consciousness rather abruptly, and was suddenly aware of all sorts of questions and possibilities hitherto closed to her." With this new consciousness came Virginia's tendency to analyze and reason through the important relationships in her life. Vanessa later wrote:

> I remember one evening as we were jumping about naked, she and I, in the bathroom, she suddenly asked me which I liked best, mother or father. Such a question seemed to me rather terrible; surely one ought not to ask it ... However, being asked, one had to reply, and I found I had little doubt as to my answer. 'Mother', I said, and she went on to explain why she, on the whole, preferred my father. I don't think, however, her preferences were quite as sure and simple as mine. She had considered both critically and had more or less analysed her feelings for them which I, at any rate consciously, had never attempted. This seemed to begin an age of much freer speech between us. If one could criticise one's parents, what or whom could one not criticise? (Stape, 6)

Early in her life, Virginia began her process of analysis of people and relationships. The dynamic created with Vanessa, as confidante and fellow investigator of life, was one that lasted throughout their lives. Virginia generally took to understanding things through verbalization, whether it be writing or speaking with her husband, her sister, or another very close friend.

As they grew up, the children also gathered together in the writing of *The Hyde Park Gate News*, a small serial newspaper written mostly to impress their parents. In it, Virginia and Thoby provided most of the writing and Vanessa the illustrations. They covered daily events, made announcements, caricatured, and the like. According to biographer, Hermione Lee,

> The tone of the *Hyde Park Gate News* ... is satirical and ruthlessly anti-emotional. Maternal feelings are travestied ('It must be hard for the Mother to see her sons growing

older and older and then to watch them leave the sweet
world of childhood behind"), ridiculous adults are mocked
(General Beadle, who says things like "it was almost too hot
but that it was pleasant to perspire freely"), and boring
visitors are dismissed (Sir Fred Pollack and his better half
arrived. We will not however say much about them as they
were not very interesting") (Lee, 107).

The paper also contained serial love stories, where the children brutally
satirized, romantic love, and horror stories, which seemed to particularly
delight Virginia. The paper as a whole provided the children with a
place to be precocious and outrageous without fear of parental reprisal.
This freedom of writing and by extension conversing excited in Virginia
a life-long love for irreverent and gossip-riddled conversation. It also
signaled her obsessive concern with the response of her audience.

Despite the fun the children had at Hyde Park Gate, it was still a
dark and dull second to the summers that they spent at Talland House,
their house by the sea in Cornwall. As an adult, it was to Talland House
that she attributed her earliest and finest memories:

> If life has a base that it stands upon, if it is a bowl that one
> fills and fills and fills—then my bowl without a doubt stands
> upon this memory. It is of lying half asleep, half awake, in
> bed in the nursery at St. Ives. It is of hearing the waves
> breaking, one, two, one, two, and sending a splash of water
> over the beach; and then breaking, one, two, one, two,
> behind a yellow blind. It is of hearing the blind draw its little
> acorn across the floor as the wind blew the blind out. It is of
> lying and hearing this splash and seeing this light, and
> feeling, it is almost impossible that I should be here; of
> feeling the purest ecstasy I can conceive (Woolf, *Sketch*,
> 64–65).

Talland House, and the summers in St. Ives, became places of family
legend, where the children remembered their parents most happily.
Still, when Virginia resurrected the place in *To the Lighthouse*, the effect
was one of both beauty and melancholy. The children bitterly resented
their father for his attention to all things scholarly, for his demand for

sympathy and affection, for his unreasonable abuses of their mother's time, for his inattentiveness to them. The book also brought forth the beauty of their mother, her own peculiar powers of attraction and absence. The children of this book bear a marked resemblance to all of the Stephen siblings. When Vanessa read the book in 1927, she wrote to Virginia:

> It seemed to me that the first part of the book you have given a portrait of mother which is more like her to me than anything that I could ever have conceived possible. It is almost painful to have her so raised from the dead. You have made one feel the excruciating beauty of her character, which must be the most difficult thing in the world to do.... You have given father too I think as clearly.... (Lee, 473–474)

The house also served as an early illustration of Virginia's attachment to place, an idea with which she struggled, wanting at once to be free of the burden of place and desperately craving a home as a way to create and recreate herself, as the move from Kensington to Bloomsbury did.

DEATH, LOSS, AND BREAKDOWN

For Virginia, her childhood seemed to end very abruptly on May 5, 1895 when her mother died at age forty-nine. Throughout her life, Virginia would continue to be haunted by that death. As an adult, she wrote of her mother's last day, remembering that her half-brother George took the children into the sickroom to say good-bye just as Leslie Stephen fled the room, racing past the outstretched arms of his youngest daughter, leaving her with the sensation of having lost both a mother and, in a smaller, more intimate way, a father. When Virginia entered the room, she registered its physical details and the nurse who sat crying after only a day's acquaintance with the deceased. Virginia remembered wanting to laugh, a famous moment of literary verisimilitude. She leaned over to kiss her mother's cheek, which still held the warmth of her body. Then she left, noting dispassionately, "'I feel nothing whatever.'" When she later returned to the room with her half-sister, Stella, her response changed slightly. She remembered the cold feeling of her mother's skin, crying, and telling Stella that she thought she saw a man sitting beside her mother. Woolf herself acknowledged that she could not determine whether this was an attempt at gaining attention or an actual vision of sorts. She was woefully unprepared to deal with the loss, as was her father.

Shortly after Julia's death, Leslie Stephen began his biography of her, a canonization of sorts that the children referred to as *The Mausoleum Book*. It became a way for Leslie to retreat from his children more deeply into his attention-grabbing grief. Virginia's half-sister, Stella, always devoted to her deceased mother, began to assume her persona, tending to the household, placating Stephen, and watching over the children, who retreated into an uneasy grief, uninformed and untutored in the ways to release emotion. They might follow the example of their controlled mother or their vitriolic father. For Virginia, as for the others, neither was possible, and she fell instead into a period of intense "intelligibility", then deep depression and eventual breakdown. She felt herself after the death able to feel and understand at a high pitch, an almost surreal awareness/understanding of the potential of things, their vivid properties. All life became overwhelmingly intense, increasing the excitement of an already overwrought young girl. It manifested itself physically with a racing pulse, feelings of "anger, terror and excitement" (Lee, 132), and a two-year period of "physical distress". A few months after the funeral, Leslie gave up the lease on St. Ives, orphaning the children in a second way from their beloved summer home, the place of some of their most vivid memories of their mother.

During this time, Virginia was left in the care of Stella, a young woman, beautiful like her mother, but possessing a somewhat gentler temperament. She was well thought of, proper and caring, and in love with a young man named Jack Hills, who would later marry her—after a period of courtship frustrated initially by Stella's devotion to Julia, and after her death, by the selfish machinations of Leslie Stephen, who did not want to lose his able housekeeper and sympathetic ear. For Virginia, the couple provided an early and idealistic view of love. Both Vanessa and Virginia were entranced by the couple, waiting up at night for them to come in, plying Stella with questions about the nature of love. Unfortunately, they were also present to hear Stephen rail against Stella, asserting that she was deserting him at his most weak, that she was taking him to the poor house when she presented the weekly accounts, that she was selfish in wanting to live in another house with her future husband. Though Leslie gave his consent to the marriage, he took a long time to soften towards the couple, and his behavior became the basis for many of Virginia's Victorian patriarchs, such as those in *A Room of One's Own*, *The Years*, and *Night and Day*.

Unfortunately, Virginia's period of difficulty was only to get worse. As Virginia recovered from the death of her mother, Stella was courted intensely by Jack Hills over the summer of 1896, culminating in a trip to Bognor in February of 1897 for Stephen, Adrian, Virginia, Vanessa, Stella, and Jack Hills, who was recovering from a small surgery. That same month, Virginia was allowed to begin taking lessons again after months of mental rest. Stella and Jack married in April, and by the end of the month, Stella had fallen ill with what was eventually diagnosed as peritonitis, although there is some conjecture as to whether an inverted uterus was to blame. At any rate, after three months of suffering, Stella received an operation on July 18, which proved unsuccessful. She died the next day, taking whatever new balance had been achieved after Julia's death with her. Virginia, once again, found herself motherless and terrified. It was an eighteen-year-old Vanessa who tried to fill the gap this time; however, while she may have done much for her sister, she drove her father to distraction.

For a few years, Stephen had been slowly becoming both increasingly deaf and increasingly querulous. With guests, he would hold an ear trumpet to his head, trying in vain to hear, or if he did not care for the company, he mumbled loudly under his breath about their merit as conversationalists or simply uttered, in a stage whisper, the desire for them to leave. In addition to these embarrassing displays, he turned the daily accounts over to Vanessa, ordering her to his study to be interrogated and then assailed with accusations that she was driving him to poverty, and that she cared little for him or the family. When he demanded sympathy, Vanessa stood silent before him, unyielding in the face of his demands. As the scenes got uglier, Vanessa came to hate Stephen, and with her hatred, Virginia began to feel ambivalent. On the one hand, her father was perhaps the person in her world who most attracted her—he was literary, aloof, intelligent, well-read, encouraging, and fascinating—but with the death of her mother and then her half-sister, Vanessa was the last female constant in her life, and

Leslie was shamelessly abusing her. Virginia wanted to support her sister and hate her father, but she found herself torn, and that weighed heavily upon her.

Around this time, Virginia began to take classes at King's College, London, partly due to her own fascination, partly to keep up with Vanessa, who was in art school, and Adrian at lessons; and partly so that she might have a worthy topic to discuss with her brother Thoby, who now attended Trinity College, Cambridge, with Leonard Woolf, Lytton Strachey, Saxon Sydney-Turner, and Clive Bell, all of whom would play a role in Virginia's life. Virginia spent many hours listening to her brother's descriptions of his brilliant friends. Between 1899 and 1904, the men had become friends; some due to their involvement with a secret society at Cambridge called the Apostles, others due to their allegiance to philosopher and teacher G.E. Moore, and others due to their attendance at Clive Bell's play reading society.

As Thoby was developing the friendships that would affect the whole family, Virginia was reading copiously during this period: Macauley; Pepys; Montaigne; Lamb's *Essays of Elia*; Lockhart's *Life of Scott*; Elizabethan writers, particularly Richard Hakluyt; the essays of her godfather, James Russell Lowell; Washington Irving; *The Scarlet Letter*; *Villette*; *Alton Locke*; *Adam Bede*; *Barchester Towers*; *Felix Holt*. In 1899, she took up bookbinding, a pursuit that would later serve her when she and Leonard developed Hogarth Press. During that same year, she took lessons in Greek and Latin with Walter Pater's sister, Clara, moving on the next year to lessons with Janet Case, with whom Virginia would have a strong friendship. Case's tutelage was rigorous and provided Virginia with ample topics to discuss with Thoby. In addition to her friendship with Case, she also became close to several women from Kensington, women generally thought to be acceptable by the extended family. Kitty Lushington, a South Kensington girl, married Leo Maxse, and provided the model for Clarissa Dalloway. She was a socialite with all the sundry social graces who eventually died in what was suspected to be suicide. Virginia also became close to her cousins, Emma and Marny Vaughn, who summered with the family, although she dropped them soon after leaving Kensington. She met and adored Emma's sister-in-law, Madge Symonds, a vivacious, romantic figure who provided Virginia a model of a working author and the inspiration for Sally Seton of *Mrs. Dalloway*. Violet Dickinson also became a part of

Virginia's life; an imposing woman at six feet two inches, she was thought to be good for Virginia—a mother figure in her thirties, kind, generous and well-liked. Most of these friendships would end or weaken as Virginia became more entrenched in her new life in Bloomsbury and more established as a writer. They became to her reminders of a more staid past, the Victorian manners and lifestyle that she had willfully left behind. The reminders were unwelcome (Lee, 157–170).

DEATH AND MADNESS

When Virginia's father, Leslie Stephen, died in 1904, these women circled round Virginia. His descent began in 1900; in 1902, the doctors diagnosed bowel cancer, but Dr. George Seton, now famous for his poor treatment of various members of the Stephen family, Virginia included, decided to wait on surgery; and by the time surgery was actually performed, in December of that year, little could be done. By Christmas, Stephen was unable to recite his traditional Milton, and he passed away on February 22, 1904. Depressed and grief-stricken, the Stephen children made plans to move to Bloomsbury. They went to Manorbrier with George Duckworth, then on holiday in Italy and Paris; throughout Virginia wrote to both Emma and Violet (who met them in Florence and continued with them to Paris, where they also met Clive Bell). In the letters, she was desperate, believing that she had not loved her father enough, that she was meant to live a life of tragedy, with people dying around her. She was beginning what would be a time of very serious mental ill health, a time of 'madness,' when she would try to kill herself, when her whole life would radically change. In this year, she also met her future husband, as Vanessa met hers, and she secured her first publication.

By May, Virginia was under the care of Dr. Savage and a team of three nurses. Her physical symptoms had intensified. She had headaches, heard voices, refused to eat. She had little control over what she said or did, and she viewed her nurses as enemies. Violet Dickinson stepped in to help in August, taking Virginia to her house at Burnham Wood. While there, Virginia threw herself out a window—her first attempt at suicide. The window was low, and Virginia was not seriously hurt, but her family and friends were further convinced of her madness. According to her nephew and biographer, Quentin Bell, "It was here too that she lay in bed, listening to the birds singing in Greek and imagining that King Edward VII lurked in the azaleas using the foulest possible language." It was not until August that a frail Virginia was able to leave with Vanessa, who took her to Teversal in Nottinghamshire. Here, she was allowed a little exercise, some letter writing, and not much else. In the fall, the siblings decided that the chaos of moving would be too much for her, and they sent her to stay with their aunt Caroline Amelia at Cambridge. Virginia was beginning to feel left out. She did not get to say good-bye to Hyde Park Gate; nor did she get the chance to put her stamp on the new house. In letters to Violet, she wrote that she was ready to begin writing again, but doctors warned her against it. Finally, some relief came through F.W. Maitland, her father's biographer.

Although Maitland initially approached Thoby, Virginia was the one who accepted the task of sifting through Leslie and Julia's letters to provide tactful excerpts for the "Life" that Maitland was writing. In addition, he asked that Virginia give a sense of her father's familial relations. This was to be her first publication, though she was cautioned against it by Jack Hills, who was still coming to the house even after the death of Stella and Leslie Stephen. Hills had forged an affection for Vanessa which horrified the family. He told Virginia that he felt she might not select wisely. Virginia was grievously insulted and responded that she "cared 10, 000 times more for delicacy and reserve where her parents were concerned than he could." She further suggested that he air whatever problems he might have with her judgment to Maitland; she would hear no more (Leaska, 100).

As Virginia's irritation with her situation in Cambridge became more intense, Vanessa finally allowed Virginia to come to London for ten days at the new house in Gordon Square. During this time, she began an important relationship via Violet Dickinson, who introduced her to Kathleen Lyttleton, the editor of the Women's Supplement of *The Guardian*. Here Virginia published her first articles, a review and an article on Haworth, the Brontë parsonage. Virginia started to work as a stringer for the paper, providing regular reviews and articles. After ten days, Virginia was sent off to their cousin Will Vaughn, who was the headmaster at Giggleswick School in Yorkshire. Here she again met Madge Symonds, who seemed subdued by the marriage and her husband's patriarchal conventions, a shadow of the formerly dynamic woman whom Virginia had idolized. From Giggleswick, Virginia returned briefly to London, back to Cambridge, then to an aunt's cottage in New Forrest. Finally, at the beginning of 1905, after a successful visit with Dr. Savage in which he declared her "completely cured," she was allowed to begin her life at Gordon Square.

A History of Abuse

When Virginia left Kensington in 1904, she also left behind a house in which she had suffered sexual molestation at the hands of her two-half brothers, George and Gerald Duckworth. For most of her life, she didn't speak of the occurrences except as vague asides in letters exchanged with Vanessa and other close friends, but when Virginia found herself immersed in the biography of Roger Fry in 1939, she began a piece entitled "A Sketch of the Past" as a respite from that work. In the piece, Virginia wrote vividly of an encounter with Gerald Duckworth which may very well have led to many of her problems regarding her body and her own sexual nature:

> There was a slab outside the dining room door for standing dishes upon. Once when I was very small Gerald Duckworth lifted me onto this, and as I sat there he began to explore my body. I can remember the feel of his hand going under my clothes; going firmly and steadily lower and lower. I remember how I hoped that he would stop; how I stiffened and wriggled as his hand approached my private parts. But it did not stop. His hand explored my private parts too. I remember resenting, disliking it—what is the word for so dumb and mixed a feeling? It must have been strong, since I still recall it. This seems to show that a feeling about certain parts of the body; how they must not be touched; how it is wrong to allow them to be touched; must be instinctive. It proves that Virginia Stephen was not born 25th January 1882, but was born many thousands of years ago; and had from the very first to encounter instincts already acquired by thousands of ancestresses in the past (Woolf, *Sketch*, 69).

The excerpt suggests several things; obviously there is a history of abuse, and equally obvious is the kind of damage that it might do the psyche of a small child. Later in life, Virginia would suffer from a reputation and, as her letters to Leonard suggest, a reality, as a sexually cold woman, as a shy spinster, a virginal goddess of sorts—and this talk came from her closest friends, including Leonard Woolf, Lytton Strachey, and Vanessa Bell, among others. Additionally, the rhetoric is interesting in that Woolf uses the phrase "how it is wrong to allow them to be touched," causing speculation as to whether Virginia blamed herself for the abuse, never fully blaming her half-brother until later in life via the memoir club, and even then, the ever-present bravado she showed in front of her witty friends may well have hidden a more private belief that she herself was partially to blame. Finally, it shows Virginia's adherence to her history as being distinctly female; she cites 'ancestresses' rather than "ancestors," implying that her intuition is based on many lives as a woman, and that women were/are the ones to suffer abuses, always. Indeed, one of the greatest internal battles she would fight would be between the intuition and emotional forbearance inherited from her mother and the pure reason, the elitism of intellect, from her father.

Later, during her adolescence, she was again molested by one of her stepbrothers. This time the perpetrator was George, an amiable, good-looking social climber, intent on bringing his poor-relation half-sisters out into the proper circles of the London social scene as much for their own benefit as his. Being seen as a benefactor to two such beautiful young women could only earn him more invitations to the better houses with which George was obsessed. He initially thought to bring Vanessa out into the scene, paying for new dresses and social outings to dinners, the opera, the theatre, anything that fashionable young people might be seen doing. Vanessa tired of the whole affair very quickly, disliking its airs of pretension and the seemingly endless discussions of nothing of great import. Despite her dislike and protestations, the agony continued for a year before Vanessa simply refused to leave the carriage which had brought them to a particular party. When Vanessa refused to play companion to George after that night, he turned to Virginia to take her place, coming into the school room early in the morning to deliver the gift of a bauble, a fondle, and an invite. She responded to the implicit pressure George provided as a benefactor. Would all gifts, money, and help of aid be rescinded should George take offense? Virginia might have also thought it potentially fun to go out. As a watcher of people, she may have suspected that the glitter of the social life might be fascinating, with all its games and machinations.

Unfortunately, that was not the case at all. Virginia felt frightened and shy, and when she became frightened, she would talk nervously; at one dinner party she rather famously discussed, at length, her feelings regarding Plato and the need to express emotion (Woolf, *Moments of Being*, 174). The two older ladies present were not impressed, and Virginia was left embarrassed, unaware that in these circles, ladies, particularly young ladies, were to be seen and not heard. The evening continued with a jaunt to the theatre to see some French actors. Mortified with her own earlier behavior, Virginia stared at her hands during the performance until she realized that the ladies beside her were covering their mouths in horror:

> I looked at the stage. To my great astonishment the lady leapt over the back of a sofa; the gentleman followed her. Round and round the stage they dashed, the lady shrieking, the man groaning and grunting in pursuit. It was a fine piece of realistic acting. As the pursuit continued, the ladies beside me held to the arms of their stalls with claws of iron. Suddenly, the actress dropped exhausted upon the sofa, and the man with a howl of gratification, loosening his clothes quite visibly, leapt on top of her. The curtain fell ... And as our procession made its way down the stalls I saw Arthur Crane leap up in his seat like a jack-in-the-box, amazed and considerably amused that George Duckworth and Lady Carnarvon of all people should have taken a girl of eighteen to see the French actors copulate upon the stage (Woolf, *Moments*, 175).

The group did not stay for the second act. George decided after parting company with the two elder ladies that Virginia still needed practice in polite society and took her to a party to socialize with aging Victorians. The evening ended more poorly still: Virginia had gone to her room for the night, undressed, and lain in bed, and was nearly asleep when she heard the creaking of the floor. She cried out to see who it was:

> "Don't be frightened", George whispered. "And don't turn

on the light, oh beloved. Beloved—" and he flung himself on my bed, and took me in his arms. Yes, the old ladies of Kensington and Belgravia never knew that George Duckworth was not only father and mother, brother and sister to those poor Stephen girls; he was their lover also. (Woolf, *Moments*, 177).

The memoir seems to make very clear that George was a sexual aggressor in the Stephen household, even as their father lay several floors below, slowly dying. Still, when Virginia wrote the sketch for the Memoir Club somewhere in 1920–21, based on a conversation that she records with Maynard Keynes, there is a suggestion which brings up the troubling notion that the memoir may not be wholly true, but contrived to impress the members of the Club. She writes of Keynes in the May 26th, 1921, entry of *A Writer's Diary*, "'The best thing that you ever did,' he said, 'was your Memoir on George. You should pretend to write about real people and make it all up.' I was dashed of course (and Oh dear what nonsense for if George is my climax I'm a mere scribbler)." But, in a letter to Ethel Smyth of February 2, 1932, she writes "I'll copy out an old memoir that tumbled out of a box when I was looking for something else, that I wrote ten years ago about our doings with George Duckworth when we were so to speak virgins." Throughout her life, Virginia seemed to view George as silly and overblown but mostly harmless. He did try to help during the times of her illness, but the memoir leaves ample room for a more sinister reading of the overwrought George and the damage he may have inflicted upon both Virginia and Vanessa, leading both to troubled sexual lives in a very different ways.

BLOOMSBURY

When the Stephen children moved to Bloomsbury and 46 Gordon Square, they sold much of the heavy Victorian furniture of Hyde Park Gate, ridding themselves of both the ideas and the accoutrements of a Kensington household. In the new house, there was color, light, pictures, and above all, a sense of freedom from the strictures of family and the old patriarchy under which they had lived. George Duckworth had married that year, releasing them from the fear that he might make it to the new life with them. Thoby was reading for the Bar, Adrian studying at Cambridge, and Vanessa under the demanding tutelege of Henry Tonks at Slade. Meanwhile, Virginia was busy reading and writing and 'street-haunting.' The Bloomsbury neighborhood provided her with ample new material; unlike Kensington, most of the people and their happenings were alien to her. She could create the details of lives as she liked, and she could practice her descriptive skills in her diary. Around her, the first motorbuses in London were lumbering down the streets, Albert Einstein was finishing his *special theory of relativity*, and Henri Matisse was beginning the Fauvist movement in art. Forster published *Where Angels Fear to Tread*, Shaw *Major Barbara*, and Edith Wharton *The House of Mirth*. Everywhere around the Stephen children, things were changing.

Awash with their freedom, they began to make dates for themselves. Thoby scheduled Thursday evenings with his Cambridge friends Lytton Strachey (a writer/historian), Clive Bell (an art critic), Saxon Sydney-Turner (a civil servant), Desmond McCarthy (a journalist/editor), Leonard Woolf (a writer, publisher, and civil servant), Maynard Keynes (an economist), and Duncan Grant (an artist). The group members changed over time, but these men were thought to be at its center. E.M. Forster was a peripheral figure, and others joined the group later: Dora Carrington (painter), Vita Sackville-West (writer), Ottoline Morrell (hostess, patron), Bertrand Russell (philosopher, essayist), and Gerald Brennan (writer), among others—but they are nowhere near as integral as these originating members. These were young men with whom both Vanessa and Virginia were acquainted through a May Ball at Cambridge prior to their father's death, through their trip to Paris, and through various visits at the house in Hyde Park Gate. Still the girls were not entirely comfortable, partly due to their own social awkwardness, exacerbated by George's jaunts around town, and partly because Thoby had so emphatically talked up his friends. Virginia recalls in "Old Bloomsbury" Thoby describing them:

> "There's an astonishing fellow called Bell", Thoby would begin directly he came back. "He's a sort of mixture between Shelley and a sporting country squire." ... Bell had never opened a book till he came to Cambridge, Thoby said. Then he suddenly discovered Shelley and Keats and went nearly

mad with excitement. He did nothing but spout poetry and write poetry. Yet he was a perfect horseman—a gift which Thoby enormously admired—and kept two or three hunters up at Cambridge.... The 'Strache' [Lytton Strachey] was the essence of culture.... He had French pictures in his room. He had a passion for Pope. He was exotic, extreme in every way—Thoby described him—so long, so thin that his thigh was no thicker than Thoby's arm.... And then Thoby, leaving me enormously impressed and rather dazed, would switch off to tell me about another astonishing fellow—a man who trembled perpetually all over. ... He was a Jew. When I asked why he trembled, Thoby somehow made me feel that it was a part of his nature—he was so violent, so savage; he so despised the whole human race.... And then perhaps the talk got upon Sydney-Turner. According to Thoby, Sydney-Turner was an absolute prodigy of learning. He had the whole of Greek literature by heart. There was practically nothing in any language that was any good that he had not read. He was very silent and thin and odd.... Sydney-Turner was the most brilliant talker he knew because he always spoke the truth (Woolf, *Moments*, 187–189).

On Thursday evenings, these men shuffled into the parlor, lowered themselves into assorted chairs, and waited for the conversation to turn in their direction. Topics were offered, then dropped after a moment, until someone would stumble onto a matter of 'truth' or 'beauty,' then the evening would begin to build as argument after argument formed, one on top of the other, until at the very crest of the talk, Saxon Sydney-Turner declared the final word on the subject. For Virginia, the talks were life-altering. Here was a place where she could be more than an attractive girl, she could be intelligent, intellectual, investigative, and open. Some of the men were openly homosexual; the others seemed asexual; the commodity, for the first time, rather than marital attractiveness, was pure intellect. Virginia describes the feeling in "Old Bloomsbury,": It seemed incredible that any of these men should want to marry us or that we should want to marry them.... When I looked round the room at 46 I thought—if you will excuse me for saying so— that I had never seen young men so dingy, so lacking in physical splendor as Thoby's friends" (191). These first impressions were shared by the old guard of Kensington. Kitty Maxse was horrified, as were Henry James and other family friends. Vanessa took to ignoring them utterly, while Virginia felt pulled between them, though she ultimately chose the disheveled young men.

Though quiet and shy at first, both Virginia and Vanessa began to actively contribute to the conversations, talking late into the night about things they found intellectually exhilarating, although Virginia often found herself annoyed with the self-satisfaction of the Cambridge crowd. Before long, Vanessa wanted more from the conversations; as a budding painter she wanted to talk about the principles of art and color and design. She began the Friday evening club to discuss these very things. Around this same time, from 1905–1907, Virginia was investigating other intellectual opportunities. She actively wrote and reviewed for a number of magazines—*The Guardian, The Times Literary Supplement, Academy, Speaker*—and she began working for Mary Sheepshanks, as an instructor at Morley College, slotted to teach English composition. She tried composition, carefully writing out full lectures, but found that her students wanted to talk about Italy. She began to change her class to one for general history, offering the students time lines and letting them borrow books which she thought were useful. She even had both Thoby and Vanessa teach classes and take students on field trips. On the whole, Virginia did not make a particularly good teacher, but she did begin to gather some important distinctions about class from her interactions with the working class. Many of them would find their way into her novels. She was torn by the fact that she believed in the 'common reader' and yet felt a profound distance from that person. She was never truly able to reconcile her own feelings of superiority and class distinction with her belief in public education, particularly for women. She spent most of her life feeling both admiration and disdain for the doers of public works and the working class.

Still, inside the Thursday evenings, the asexual oasis was not to last. Clive Bell and Vanessa were falling for each other and would marry; Lytton, Desmond, Duncan Grant, and Maynard Keynes were in perpetual love straits, and Virginia was not outside of it; she received her own stirrings of interest from a few Cambridge men, such as Walter Headlam, Edward Hilton Young, Sydney Waterlow, and Walter Lamb.

In September of 1906, Virginia found herself having to deal with the impending loss of her sister Vanessa to the intimacy of marriage, a sphere from which Virginia felt profoundly excluded, and her brother to typhoid fever.

The Stephen children decided to go on vacation, to visit the sights of Greece. The brothers left early, to take the adventurous route, via Trieste, sailing down the Dalmatian coast and traveling through Montenegro on horseback. For Thoby, this was to be the end of his days as a student. He was going to be a professional upon his return, and the trip would be a "last hurrah." His sisters were set to meet him and Adrian in Greece. For Virginia, the trip was meant to be the culmination of her Greek studies, where the language, the literature, and the antiquities she had studied would all come together; she would see the bridge between classical Greece and the country it had become. For Vanessa, it was a chance to escape the question of marriage to Clive, one that had been hounding her for more than a year. With them went Violet Dickinson, in the role of den mother.

Virginia kept diaries throughout the trip, trying to articulate all that she was seeing. In many entries, she is overwhelmed, without words for what she saw. All around her she felt the palimpsest of the ancient with the actual. In spite of her awe, the trip was troubled by illness from the beginning. Vanesa began to feel ill on the voyage over, and they had to stop in Corinth so that she might recover a little before they carried on to Athens. In Athens, she got worse. Violet stayed behind to tend her while Virginia and her brothers moved on to Euboea. When they returned, Vanessa was worse still. The doctors diagnosed her with appendicitis, which was compounded by Vanessa's stress and depression. They carried on to Constantinople, though Vanessa was beside herself with pain. On October 14, Thoby, ill, returned to London; his siblings returned on November 1, a sick Violet Dickinson with them. She returned to her home in Manchester Street for the duration of her illness, and Virginia and Vanessa returned home to find Thoby in bed with a high fever, diagnosed by the family doctor as malaria. Ten days later, they realized that the diagnosis was false. Like the ailing Violet, Thoby had typhoid. On November 17, he was operated on; by November 20, he was dead at twenty-six years years of age.

For Virginia, it was like losing her father again. Thoby had become her intellectual mentor. He had led her through her Greek and offered her the benefit of his own formal schooling (a schooling which Virginia deeply desired for herself). The character of her brother came back to her throughout her life as Jacob of *Jacob's Room* and through her lifelong associations with his closest friends, her love of Greek, her struggle with aetheism. For several weeks after Thoby's death, Virginia was still keeping him alive via letters that she was sending to the gravely ill Violet Dickinson. Worried that the shock and sorrow of Thoby's death would impede and even harm the recovery of her friend, she wrote letters of her dead brother's supposed antics, flirting with nurses, recovering a little, cursing, demanding particular foods, arguing with the people around him. After this death, Virginia did not break down; instead she had the opportunity to recreate Thoby as a fictional character, to regain some control over the arbitrary nature of death. Through writing, Virginia could adjust gradually to the shock of his death and keep him, in some small way, alive for herself. Violet Dickinson only discovered the news of his death when she read a review of F.W. Maitland's biography of Leslie Stephen. It mentioned the death of his eldest son, only two years after his own.

During the darkest hours of Thoby's illness, Clive Bell was omnipresent, caring for Vanessa, discussing the intricacies of the sick room with Virginia and worrying for his friend. The experience not only brought Virginia a little closer to him, it also sufficed to bring Vanessa to a marriage agreement. In the course of a few days, Virginia lost her brother to death, her sister to Clive, and the house on 46 Gordon Square to affianced couple. Each was a major blow. Suddenly, her family had shrunk to only one other, her brother, Adrian, with whom she was never very close.

In February of 1907, Clive and Vanessa Bell were married. When they returned from their honeymoon, they were joyous, and Adrian and Virginia had moved to 29 Fitzroy Square, an area slightly less respectable than Gordon Square. The houses became a competition for the most lovely. Virginia felt she could hardly compete with the 20, 000 pounds settled on Clive when he married. Fitzroy Square was shabbier, less formal, but Virginia had the whole second floor to herself. In July of that year, the Bells told Virginia that Vanessa was expecting. For Virginia, the news was a shock and yet another reminder that she was outside the circle of happiness. It became clear through correspondence with both Clive and Vanessa that Virginia's writing was meant to take the place of both marriage and children. It was to be her consolation prize. Like Leslie before her, Virginia wanted to rage against what was being taken from her, but she tried to still the instinct, only revealing it in bitter letters to Violet. She tried to join in the spirit of expectancy. She began to write "Reminiscences," a history of Vanessa, part memoir, part biography, part paean. In it, Vanessa is portrayed as beautiful and full of color. In some ways, it was Virginia's way of giving birth to her sister as a full-blown fictional character, as Thoby had become one in the letters Virginia sent to Violet after his death. At the same time, she was beginning one of the first drafts of what would eventually become *The Voyage Out*. Virginia wrote at least five complete drafts of the manuscript before it went to print.

During the years at Fitzroy Square, the members of the Cambridge crowd, of the Friday night art club, were all growing closer. Suddenly, no subject seemed taboo. There was not only talk of art and beauty; there was also talk of sex. Perhaps the most famous recorded moment of this belongs to Lytton Strachey. According to Virginia, she and Vanessa were sitting together in the parlor, with Clive soon to be entering, when

> [s]uddenly the door opened and the long and sinister figure of Mr. Lytton Strachey stood on the threshold. He pointed his finger at a stain on Vanessa's white dress.
> "Semen?" he said.
> Can one really say it? I thought & we burst out laughing. With that one word all of the barriers of reticence and reserve went down. A flood of the sacred fluid seemed to overwhelm us. Sex permeated our conversation. The word bugger was never far from our lips. We discussed copulation with the same excitement and openness that we had discussed the nature of good. It is strange to think how reticent, how reserved we had been and for how long (Bell, 124).

For Virginia, this experimentation of language was extending to her personal life, not in an expression of physical sexuality but one of a mental flirting. Both she and Clive felt distant from Vanessa in 1908 with the birth of Julian. Suddenly, Vanessa, who had been the central figure in both of their lives, was in love with someone else, and the euphoric passion of motherhood never let go of her. In its wake, Virginia, however consciously, saw a way to insinuate herself between Clive and Vanessa. She began to make tentative overtures to Clive, asking him to read her writing, an intimacy she was only to allow one other, Leonard Woolf. Clive proved an enthusiastic and insightful critic, a good friend and an ardent suitor. When Vanessa did catch glimpses of her husband and Virginia, she was dismayed at the growing infatuation, but could do little to stop it. The flirtation flourished in both Virginia's home in Cornwall and on vacation with the Bells in Italy in September of that year.

In 1909, Virginia's strange and strained love life became even stranger when, in February of that year, Lytton Strachey, a flamboyant, gossipy, and practicing homosexual, asked Virginia to marry him. Confounding them both still more, Virginia accepted. Lytton immediately became terrified that she would try to kiss him. He let a night pass, considering the horror of marrying a heterosexual woman, while Virginia considered the idea of marrying a man who would put no sexual demands on her, but who also would not love her wholly. By the next day, the two agreed to forget that the affair had ever happened. Still, Strachey, ever talkative, felt compelled to draft a letter to Leonard Woolf in Ceylon, telling him that he had proposed, and that while he realized that marriage to Virginia was not for him, it may well be perfect for Leonard. Leonard apparently agreed, as he was slowly being convinced by Strachey and by his own experience with Virginia, and perhaps his own homesickness, that marriage to Virginia would mean "perfect happiness."

In that same year, Virginia met Ottoline Morrell for the first time, lunching with her and finding her strange, fascinating, and somewhat pathetic. Ottoline was a flamboyant woman, a large personality with an outrageous mode of dress. Virginia wrote of her to Madge Vaughn: "[Ottoline] has the head of a Medusa; but she is very simple and innocent in spite of it, and worships the arts" (Lee 272). Indeed, she was rabid about artists and rich, a member of the peerage ready to patronize the Bloomsbury crowd, particularly Virginia. It was the beginning of a long association that brought together artists, writers, and other bohemians and intellectuals.

NATIONALLY KNOWN SUBVERSIVES

In 1910, the Bloomsbury group would begin to make national headlines, not as artists, but as troublemakers. Adrian Stephen, in February of that year, decided to enact an elaborate hoax on the British Navy. He and a friend, William Horace de Vere Cole, decided to dress up as the Emperor of Abyssinia and his entourage, and tour the newest warship in His Majesty's Fleet. They dressed up in turbans and robes, blackened their faces, applied fake moustaches, and took the train from Paddington to Weymouth, practicing their Swahili on the way. When they arrived, a red carpet awaited them, complete with a naval band, a launch to the ship and an honor guard. Adrian had sent a telegram ahead, notifying Admiral William May of their impending visit; he and Commander William Fisher, a Stephen cousin, took them around the ship. While there, the group spoke broken Virgil, Swahili, and a series of phrases, "bunga bunga" and "chuck-a-choi, chuck-a-choi" being the most famous. When offered food, they claimed religious reasons for declining (although it is probable that they feared the fate of their fake facial hair) they refused a twenty-one gun salute and finally returned to shore. On the train back to Paddington, they were given white-glove service. The joke made national news and colored Bloomsbury as the worst kind of public miscreants, defiling the dignity of the Navy, its practices and national defense, cross-dressing and gender-bending. Though all had sworn to secrecy, Cole chose to inform the Foreign Office in person of the hoax. They were not amused; nor was the extended Stephen family. Letters of outrage poured in from aunts, uncles, and other members of the old guard. Adrian and Virginia were soiling the family name, particularly Virginia, an unmarried woman behaving in such a fashion. Virginia added her own final note on the event in 1940:

> About a week or two later the real Emperor of Abyssinia arrived in London. He complained that wherever he went in the street boys ran after him calling out Bunga Bunga. And when he asked the first Lord of the Admiralty whether he might visit the Channel Flight, Mr. McKenna replied that he regretted to inform his Majesty that it was quite impossible. (Lee, 280)

Despite the frivolities, trouble was brewing with Virginia. The year 1910 came with a period of illness, one that would last on and off through World War I, buffered from the world's violence by her own illness. In January, the Bells met Roger Fry on a train. They became fast friends, and Fry was to play an integral part in getting Virginia to agree to treatment. By March, Virginia was in the middle of a breakdown, with headaches, insomnia, tension and a refusal to eat. The Bells took her to Studland to recuperate. She returned to Fitzroy Square in mid-April, but her recovery was illusory. Her symptoms began to reassert themselves with greater force. The Bells rented a house in Canterbury and took Virginia there to rest, but after two weeks, a pregnant Vanessa found that her unstable sister was too much for her to handle with her pregnancy. She went to London to seek the advice of Dr. George Savage, their family doctor. They decided to send Virginia to a home for the privileged and insane called Burley Park, run by a Miss Jean Thomas. Vanessa wrote ahead to Virginia to let her know of the decision, and Virginia left reluctantly for the home on June 30. She remained there until August 10, cursing Vanessa, and getting to know Jean Thomas, whom she was charming. At the end of her incarceration, she went on a walking tour of Cornwall, accompanied by the sympathetic and watchful Thomas. In September, she returned to Studland to be with the Bells and their new baby, Quentin, and by November, she had returned to work on *The Voyage Out*. At the same time, Roger Fry was astonishing and discomfiting London with the first Post-Impressionist Exhibit at the Grafton Gallery. He had worked formerly for the Metropolitan Museum of Art as its British Advisor and would become the leader of a major English movement, the Omega Workshop, which had at its center Fry, Vanessa Bell, and Duncan Grant.

In December of 1910, Virginia found a house in Firle, near Lewes, that she called Little Talland House, in memory of her childhood summer home by the sea. She spent the beginning of 1911 with Vanessa decorating and finishing her new home; she was firmly entrenched by March, working on her book and taking long walks. In April, Virginia suddenly had another scare. She received a wire from Clive Bell and Roger Fry. They were in Constantinople, and Vanessa was ill from a miscarriage. Put immediately in mind of her brother Thoby, Virginia rushed to Constantinople, where she and Roger Fry nursed Vanessa back to health. It became clear in the sick room that Vanessa and Fry had

fallen in love, that Clive and Vanessa were to be companions only, and for the rest of their lives. With Vanessa newly occupied with someone else, Virginia no longer felt any attraction for Clive instead, she was very much attracted to Roger. With Roger, however, the attraction was different. He was not the sort to engage in petty flirting to upset Vanessa. His appeal was of a more paternal sort, the trusted male figure which she had wanted from her father, which he had failed to give. The friendship between Virginia and Fry was quick to develop and long-lasting. She eventually wrote his biography.

June 1911 was a good month for Virginia—Leonard Woolf came back into her life in full force. While Virginia had been writing at Gordon Square and Fitzroy Square, Leonard was working for the Colonial Civil Service in Ceylon, "keeping order with a stick over 40, 000 Arab and Tamil pearl-fishers at Marichukaddi, improving the salt collection rate in Hambantota Province, grappling with outbreaks of rinderpest and the opium trade, learning Tamil and Sinhalese, streamlining the census-taking operations, riding and cycling many miles through the jungle, and experimenting with new methods in ploughing, cotton-growing, and education" (Lee, 293). Leonard found himself increasingly disgusted by the colonial system, so much so that he referred to himself as "the buffoon in a vast comic opera" (Lee, 293). As a boy, Woolf grew up in Kensington, the same neighborhood as Virginia. His father, Sidney, was a barrister, and his mother the daughter of a diamond merchant from Amsterdam. On his father's side, his grandfather had put a proviso in his will that the children would only inherit if they married Jews. His grandfather was also fiercely dedicated to education, believing that it would help his children to become upwardly mobile. To an extent, it worked. Leonard Woolf grew up middle-class until his father died at the age of 48 and the family was forced to move out to the Putney suburb. Sidney Woolf had saved no money, and his son was made painfully aware of their dire straits. Leonard was eleven at the time.

Due to his own intellectual savvy, Leonard became a scholarship boy at St. Paul's and again at Cambridge in the Classics. While at Cambridge, he became a devotee of G.E. Moore, and though he learned a great deal from Moore and his views, his scholarship overall was second-rate. He did poorly on the Civil Service examination and so could only opt for the Colonial Service, as he could not teach. He went grudgingly, but Leonard Woolf turned out to be a first-rate administrator—organized, disciplined, thorough, ethical.

Physically, Leonard was slender, dark-haired, intense-looking with a near-constant tremor that worsened in times of stress, particularly social stress. His intensity and self-discipline were awesome, and crucial in both his work and his marriage to Virginia. He was constant, loyal, fiercely dedicated to social justice. He felt a devotion to family, although he was also embarrassed by his mother and her middle-class values. He explored his mixed reaction in his novel *The Wise Virgins*. He had mixed feelings about being Jewish. On the one hand, he felt keenly the history of his people and their plight and perseverance; on the other hand, he was constantly made aware of the fact that, as a Jew, he was an outsider. Antisemitism was widespread and well-accepted across England, particularly among the upper-middle class. Even Virginia felt a strong antisemitism that she did not mask from him. In letters and exchanges, many of Leonard's friends felt perfectly comfortable making antisemitic remarks, assuming because Leonard had chosen Cambridge and life with Virginia that he had exchanged his Jewish identity for a new, more mainstream identity. Others responded like Jacques Raverat, who claimed that he hated Jews "because they crucified Christ daily" (Lee, 289). Leonard was constantly an outsider throughout his life. Only with Virginia, and her great need for him, was he completely accepted.

Unbeknownst to Virginia, he had already determined to marry her and was courting her with the single-minded intensity that he brought to everything. When the lease on Fitzroy Square came up, Virginia and Adrian decided to move, and the Bloomsbury Group established itself in 38 Brunswick Square as a loosely connected group of boarders. Maynard Keynes and his lover, Duncan Grant, occupied the ground floor, Adrian the first, Virginia the second, and Leonard Woolf the top. Dinners were placed outside of doors at appointed hours and the trays returned outside of the door at appointed hours. Such a living arrangement was very modern, particularly for a young single woman. As expected, the family from Kensington was appalled, but Virginia was delighted. She worked through the week and had guests to Little Talland House on the week-end. One such guest was Leonard Woolf, with whom she found Asheham House while walking. She decided, with Vanessa, to secure the lease for 1912.

Marriage and Madness

In January of 1912, Leonard proposed marriage to Virginia. Initially, she neither refused nor accepted; like her parents before her, a series of letters were exchanged before any decisions were made. Leonard wrote to her, "I'm sure now that apart from being in love ... it would be worth the risk of everything to marry you" (Leaska, 154). Virginia fired a quick note in return, begging to go on as before and apologizing for any pain she might have caused him. Then Leonard received a letter from Vanessa, urging him to pursue Virginia, writing, "You're the only person I know whom I can imagine as her husband" (Leaska, 154). But as February progressed, Virginia's health was rapidly deteriorating, perhaps from the stress of a potential marriage, perhaps because of her novel. Many stressors were working on Virginia, and she was having a hard time fending them off; her symptoms had become so severe that she returned willingly to Burley Park with Jean Thomas on February 16. When she returned, she spent the end of February through April with Katherine ("Ka") Cox, a young, college-educated woman she had met early in 1911. Ka was embroiled in an affair with Rupert Brooke, a member of the Neo-Pagans, a group of free-living Fabians. All of this left Leonard in the unenviable position of having to ask for an extension of his leave from the Colonial Service, as he was to return to service on May 20. He cited personal reasons but did not explain further. He sent another letter to Virginia, telling her, "I wouldn't have asked you to marry me if I thought it would bring you unhappiness.... I shall never be content now with second best.... You must finish your novel first and while you are doing it you must not try to decide.... After all, I've had more happiness in the last two months than in all the rest of my life put together" (Leaska, 156). The letter was important for Virginia, as it assured her that her writing would come before anything else. Here finally was a partner who respected her as both a writer and a person. After sending this letter, Leonard received a reply from the Colonial Office, asking him for a more specific reason for his request; when he refused to give one, the Governor of Ceylon refused his request.

In the interim, he received a reply from Virginia:

It seems to me that I am giving you a great deal of pain— some in the most casual way—and therefore I ought to be as plain with you as I can.... Of course, I *can't* explain what I

feel—these are some of the things that strike me. The
obvious advantages of marriage stand in my way. I say to
myself, anyhow, you'll be quite happy with him; and he will
give you companionship, children, and a busy life—then I
say By God, I will not look upon marriage as a profession.
The only people who know of it, all think it suitable; and that
makes me scrutinise my own motives all the more. Then, of
course, I feel angry sometimes at the strength of your desire.
Possibly your being a Jew comes in also at this point. You
seem so foreign. And then I am fearfully unstable.... All I can
say is that in spite of these feelings which go chasing each
other all day long when I am with you, there is some feeling
which is permanent, and growing.... I sometimes think that
if I married you, I could have everything—and then—is it
the sexual side of it that comes between us? As I told you
brutally the other day, I feel no physical attraction in you.
There are moments—when you kissed me the other day was
one—when I feel no more than a rock. And yet your caring
for me as you do almost overwhelms me. It is so real, and so
strange ... (Lee, 305–306).

The letter foreshadows their greatest marital asset, open, intimate
conversation, and the largest obstacle in their married life: Virginia's lack
of sexual attraction for her husband. What neither seemed to realize yet
was that Virginia's only sexual interest was in women. Still, from this
reply, Leonard gained hope for his cause, and on April 25, he submitted
his resignation to the Colonial Office; the Office offered to reconsider
his request for leave but was finally forced to accept his resignation on
May 7. Later that month, when Virginia was one chapter shy of finishing
The Voyage Out, she agreed to marry Leonard—perhaps because of their
intimate friendship, perhaps because of the avid sponsorship of Lytton
and Vanessa, perhaps because the doctor told her that getting married
would be beneficial for her mental state. No one can say for sure. Most
likely it is some combination thereof.

The couple spent June and July rushing around to introduce
family and friends, and Virginia found herself tiring out. She had to spend
days resting intermittently throughout the summer. On August 12, 1912,
Leonard and Virginia Woolf were married at the Registry Office; they

honeymooned in the south of France and in Spain. When they returned home, it had been decided that the physical aspect of their marriage was not going to work. The two settled into an affectionate but largely platonic companionship.

They began their married life in a set of rooms atop an 18th century building near the Strand. The rooms came without a kitchen, and the two ate their meals at local pubs. For Virginia, this was an incredibly stressful time. In the back of her mind, she had the spectres of her mother and her half-sister, Stella, both of whom died early in their marriages. Like her father, she was undone by money troubles, and neither she nor Leonard had a steady job. He worked part-time as a secretary for the Second Post-Impressionist Exhibit with Roger Fry. She was reviewing and writing, but together they brought in relatively little money, and she found herself rushing to finish her final draft of *The Voyage Out*. In March of 1913, Virginia had finally finished her final draft, and Leonard took it to Gerald Duckworth's publishing company. It was accepted for publication on April 12. Virginia spent May and June correcting page proofs, but the stress of her new lifestyle and the pressures of publication, combined with her paranoia regarding ridicule and review, left her with headaches and insomnia; the illness that she had kept at bay was threatening to encroach on her marriage.

At the same time, Leonard was strengthening his political career, working with Margaret Llewellyn Davies of the Women's Co-operative Guild, for the cause of British Socialism, and with the Fabian Society, a socialist group committed to the slow implementation of socialism in Great Britain. With Leonard so busy and involved, Virginia found herself slipping further and further away. Upon Dr. Savage's orders, she spent July at Burley Park with Jean Thomas, but with her release in August, the symptoms had only intensified. She and Leonard traveled to Asheham, then to London, then to the Plough Inn, where they had spent the first night of their honeymoon. It didn't help. She was distraught, worried, unable to eat; Leonard called on Ka Cox to come and help. She arrived and aided Leonard in bringing Virginia back to London, where she was to see Henry Head, a doctor recommended by Roger Fry. They stayed at Adrian's rooms in Brunswick Square. On September 9, Leonard left to arrange a consultation between Head and Savage. In his haste to leave, he forgot to lock the case with the sleeping draughts. At 6:30 pm, still in Savage's office, he received a call from Ka;

Virginia had fallen into a deep sleep. He rushed home and found his wife unconscious. He called Vanessa and told her to bring the doctor. When Head arrived, he discovered that she had taken 100 grains of veronal. Maynard Keynes' brother, Geoffrey, now a doctor at St. Bartholomew's and a resident of Brunswick Square, rushed with Leonard to the hospital to get a stomach pump. They worked pumping her stomach until 1:30 in the morning. By six, she was out of danger, but she did not wake up for another 24 hours. The suicide attempt did little to calm her symptoms. The doctors called it neurasthenia. After researching the illness, Leonard believed it to be manic-depressive psychosis, a diagnosis that many believe to be accurate today.

Leonard could not put her in a private-care facility after the suicide attempt, and he was loath to put her in an asylum. His savior came in the unexpected form of George Duckworth, who offered his home, Dalingridge Hall. With nurses in tow, they made their way to George's home, where they stayed for two months before returning to Asheham in December. They would spend most of the next year at Asheham with Leonard, keeping a close watch on Virginia's slow recovery. In September, they returned to London and Virginia began reading again, writing in her diary, and taking cooking lessons. In December, while house hunting in Richmond, they found Hogarth House. On Virginia's birthday in 1915, she and Leonard decided to buy Hogarth House and a printing press, the latter as a hobby/diversion for both of them.

The respite was short-lived. She became deranged again in February, making her last journal entry on the fifteenth. She would not write in it again until August of 1917. She had no idea that the publication of *The Voyage Out* was successful and receiving strong reviews, and the World War that was raging around her was blocked by her mental state. She passed through most of the war with little understanding of its operations. She labored through her illness to discover that yet another right had been taken from her. Leonard and the doctors had decided that she would not be able to have children, that such a stressor could only overwhelm her and trigger more illness. It was a decision that hurt and haunted Virginia Woolf. Her only conception now would be intellectual.

In March, Virginia was taken to a nursing home while Leonard moved their belongings, nurses, and servants into Hogarth House. He set the press up in the basement and prepared for his wife's arrival in

April. They remained there until September, then shifted to Asheham until November. Those months were spent in relative happiness as Virginia slowly recovered.

By November, Virginia was fully cognizant of the war—the Zeppelin attacks on London and the conscription that threatened many of their friends and even Leonard. The majority of the Bloomsbury crowd was not in support of the war, due to either apathy or an actual objection to the war itself. Much of 1916 was spent trying to help her friends and family avoid war and its ravages. She wrote letters in support of Duncan Grant and his lover, David Garnett, in their attempts to avoid military service as conscientious objectors, claiming meaningful work as laborers on a fruit farm. She wrote to Vanessa Bell to convince her to bring the children with her to a farm near Charleston where she believed they would be safe. Vanessa did move to Charleston, in an uneasy love triangle with Grant and Garnett. Lytton Strachey avoided the draft due to medical reasons and Leonard Woolf due to the precarious health of his wife and his own trembling hands. The war became part of Woolf's aesthetic; images of bombs and destruction began to appear in her writing. She believed that the war had caused a schism, that it had orphaned literature. She also began to understand, as a result of wartime censorship and propaganda, the power that she and Leonard might wield with a private press.

That same year, the war, which had seemed distant in many ways, suddenly came home to the Woolfs: one of Leonard's brothers was killed by a shell and another brother wounded by the same shell. They found themselves huddling in basements with servants, forcing the always class-conscious Virginia to attempt to speak with her servants, with whom she was always uneasy, believing in more rights, better hours, better pay, more freedom and more privacy for the servants, but all the while judging their relative intellect and the ways in which they *should* have embodied certain ideas she held regarding the lower classes and their behavior. She struggled with these conflicted feelings all of her life, particularly with her servant Nelly Boxall, who came to them in 1916. At this time, Virginia was recovering and began chairing and organizing the monthly meetings of the Richmond Branch of the Women's Co-operative Guild, which she did for four years, inviting friends to speak for half an hour about social issues, venereal diseases, sexual education, and other matters of practical and political concern. She wanted the same freedom of sexual discourse for women of all classes, although in a typical show of snobbery, she noted how much more such education was necessary for the lower class than for her own.

On April 24, 1917, Virginia and Leonard's dream of owning their own press became a reality. The press they had bought in March was delivered and put in the dining room. Leonard believed that it might distract Virginia, give her something to concentrate on other than her illness and her writing. The partnership worked well. Virginia set the type and bound the books, while Leonard, with his shaky hands, worked the machining aspect of the press. Both solicited work. The first work to come from the press would come from its owners, Leonard's "Three Jews" and Virginia's "The Mark on the Wall"; it signified their partnership. For Virginia, this was the first piece of writing that she had done without the worry of a particular audience. She need not worry about acceptance; instead she was free to consider the aesthetic and narrative possibilities that she had before her. This story marked the beginning of a new style of writing for Virginia. She was moving away from the traditional narrative of *The Voyage Out* and *Night and Day* into the more experimental work for which she would become famous.

The book came out in July, accompanied by woodcuts done by an artist friend of Lytton Strachey's, Dora Carrington, a woman deeply in love and deeply devoted to the homosexual Strachey. It was the first Hogarth Press publication, and in many ways representative of Hogarth's primary strengths. First, much of what the press published came from within Bloomsbury or the Cambridge crowd or Vanessa's "neo-pagan" artist friends. Second, after the publication of *Night and Day*, all other Virginia Woolf books were published (at least initially) by Hogarth, and finally, both Virginia and Leonard used the press as a place to publish revolutionary ideas, both their own and those of others, as well as new writers who would not find publication elsewhere, Gertrude Stein and T.S. Eliot among them.

LITERARY RIVALS

Lytton Strachey also introduced Virginia to one of her greatest literary rivals and sometime friend, Katherine Mansfield. Mansfield had been at one of Ottoline Morrell's parties with Lytton and had expressed appreciation for *The Voyage Out*. Virginia, insatiable for positive feedback, agreed to meet her. Soon after they met, Virginia asked Mansfield for a story, and she delivered "Prelude," a sixty-eight-page story. The relationship was one of bitter rivalry and mutual admiration. Virginia believed that Katherine might be one of the few women on earth with whom she could seriously discuss literature and writing, but at the same time, she was one of the few women who could rival Virginia artistically. These two things made the friendship uneasy, particularly as they seem to have been mutually felt. With the size of the Mansfield manuscript, Virginia and Leonard were forced to seek the assistance of a nearby commercial printer. By July, the piece had sold three hundred copies, bringing the press an influx of cash, but Virginia found herself disillusioned in August when she read Mansfield's story "Bliss" in *The British Review*. Virginia decided that she hated the story, and she so associated the writing with the woman, she decided that she hated Katherine, too. She felt differently once she saw Mansfield again, but the love/hate relationship was never far from the boiling point, and Virginia never understood her affinity with Katherine until the latter's sudden death in January of 1923.

She also found herself in an unending rivalry with Vanessa. In December of 1918, Vanessa gave birth to another child, Angelica, the daughter of Duncan Grant, with whom she would share a tortured love affair for the rest of her life. At the time, Duncan was also intimate with David Garnett, who also lived on the farm. Garnett had the rather dubious distinction of being present at the birth of his wife, fathered by his lover. Around this same time, Clive was beginning his love affair with Mary Hutchinson, whom Virginia would draw from to create Jinny in *The Waves*. Still, at this point, Virginia's sense of rivalry was extending beyond family.

Virginia was also coming into contact with other literary lions of her day. Her friend Lytton Strachey was suddenly famous with the publication of *Eminent Victorians*, causing Virginia to furiously work at her new novel, *Night and Day*, so that she might catch up to Strachey's sudden success. In the spring of 1918, as she was writing *Night and Day*, a Miss Harriet Weaver came to pitch James Joyce's *Ulysses*. Although somewhat intrigued by it, the Woolfs were forced to pass on it, largely because of its sheer volume, but also because, after inquiries by Leonard, it was clear that no commercial press would touch the book for fear of the obscenity laws. Still, Virginia was made powerfully aware of a new voice in literature, one that she found both vulgar and threatening. Was Joyce taking her innovations in fiction? Was he doing them better? Meeting T.S. Eliot, who would become a life long friend, did nothing to alleviate this fear.

When Virginia met Tom Eliot she was taken aback at how assertive he was, how convinced of the dual glories of Ezra Pound and James Joyce. Still, she believed in the merit of his poems, and the Hogarth Press took his book *Poems*, releasing it in concordance with Virginia's experimental piece *Kew Gardens* and John Middleton Murry's *The Critic in Judgment* on May 12, 1918. *The Times Literary Supplement (TLS)* embraced *Kew Gardens* and the Woolfs were inundated with requests. A second edition was quickly brought out with the help of a commercial printer, as well as a reprint of "The Mark on the Wall." Suddenly, Virginia Woolf was becoming a bankable name, a fact noted by Duckworth and Company when they accepted *Night and Day* for publication in April.

For the pending publication of *Night and Day*, Virginia felt only apprehension; this combined with the painful loss of Asheham in February 1919 set the stage for depression. The only way to combat it was to work, and find a new home. Virginia tried to get excited about house hunting, finding first Round House in Rodmell. It was a small house, part of a windmill, that she had seen with Vanessa, and she impetuously bought it. Leonard was not impressed. She continued her search, finding a notice for Monk's House, a small house with a beautiful garden, large and untamed; she believed that the gardens would be perfect for Leonard. There were several outbuildings, too, one of which would become Virginia's writing room. Enchanted, she and Leonard bought it for seven hundred pounds. Both Leonard and Virginia delighted in the house, carefully assembling its contents from auctions, the work of Duncan Grant and Vanessa, and the furniture already in the house. Very quickly the place felt like home, and with the successes of her later novels, conveniences were added: two water closets and a bathroom with hot water, a small bedroom for Virginia and a writing studio. Monk's House was their home, to varying degrees, for the rest of their lives, a more than adequate compensation for the loss of Asheham.

Night and Day, with its pending publication in the midst of *Kew Gardens* and "A Mark," seemed strange. For the most part, the novel followed a traditional linear narrative format, not at all like the simultaneous time and emphasis on individual perception in the two shorter pieces. Some charge that Virginia was simply trying to prove to herself that she was sane, that she could write a traditional novel and with that out of the way, she could move past her self-imposed apprenticeship on to her true interests. In any case, the two shorter pieces married with a third, *An Unwritten Novel*, which she wrote in January 1920. According to Mitchell Leaska, a Woolf critic and biographer,

> [i]f Virginia Woolf could join the seperate technical methods utilized in each of her three pieces, she would achieve the freedom of mental association and interior monologue, the freedom of shifting narrative points of view, and finally the freedom to create fictional worlds built on pure narrative invention which did not promise the "Truths" of omniscient storytelling (Leaska, 212).

The hypothesis of these three pieces became the formula for her next novel, *Jacob's Room*, which she worked on steadily from May to September. At this point, Virginia was very productive, writing two to three pieces a week for the *Times Literary Supplement*, working on *Jacob's Room*, letter writing, talking with Katherine Mansfield, and jotting sketches in her journal.

Night and Day met with mixed reactions. It sold well, establishing that Woolf had an audience, but Katherine Mansfield wrote for *Athenaeum* what Virginia considered to be a nasty, vicious review:

> We had thought that this world vanished for ever, that it was impossible to find on the great ocean of literature a ship that was unaware of what has been happening; yet there is *Night and Day*, new, exquisite—a novel in the tradition of the English novel. In the midst of our admiration it makes us feel old and chill. We had not thought to look upon its like again (Leaska, 215).

Virginia, always painfully susceptible to criticism, immediately felt hurt and distanced from Katherine, yet when next they spoke, Katherine referred to the novel as "an amazing achievement"; wanting so much to like her fellow writer, Virginia was mollified. Still, the criticism stung, and Virginia felt compelled to answer the criticism with a group of new experimental works called *Monday or Tuesday*.

Despite the pain caused by the review, Virginia was still fascinated by Mansfield and her writing. She believed that it escaped the obsessive hyper-emphasized I of Joyce and other male writers of the day. In August of 1920, she wrote again in her diary of Katherine, after having said good-bye to her for the next two years, "A woman caring as I care for writing is rare enough I suppose to give me the queerest sense of echo coming back to me from her mind the second after I've spoken.... But we propose to write to each other—She will send her diary. Shall we? Will she? If I were left to myself I should; being the simpler, the more direct of the two.... Strange how little we know of our friends" (Leaska, 215). It was to be the last conversation that she had with Mansfield, though; there would be a few more letters and then silence until Mansfield's death, at which time Virginia felt mournful for her friend/rival, one of the few female writers with whom she had really connected.

In the safety of Monk's House, Virginia felt some relief from the criticism, but she was still depressed by her novel and terrified of public ridicule. After the completion of every novel, she battled depression; the only way in which she might stave it off was to work, often moving among essays, reviews, and her current novels. Such was the case with *Jacob's Room*; she believed that the work would redeem her, define her, make her valuable. Additionally, she used the book not only to recreate and thereby reconcile her dead brother, Thoby, but also to explore this new style of writing that moved beyond chronological storytelling into a more impressionistic style that tried to enact the process of being human with its associative tracks and emotional life. This was a novel of the interior, but also one that would vividly speak of the effects of World War I on a generation of young men, which she was accused of ignoring in her past novel. She worked for two years on the novel, stopping for social engagements and bouts of depression and for her experimental stories in *Monday or Tuesday*.

She also spent a great deal of time at the Press, where she and Leonard had agreed that he needed an assistant. The year 1920 was busy, particularly for Leonard, who was just beginning to flex his political and literary muscles. He worked as the editor for the international supplement of the *Contemporary Review* and "leader/editor" on foreign affairs for the *Nation* (Leaska, 213). He also published *Empire and Commerce in Africa* and was working on *Socialism and Co-operation*. He applied his energies to translating *The Notebooks of Anton Tchecov* and prepping his own *Stories from the East* for Hogarth. He was also made the Labour candidate for the Combined English Universities (213). With all of this going on, they recruited Ralph Partridge to help at the Press, a friend of Lytton's and the lover of Carrington, the third person in that strange triangle. The Woolfs found themselves in the middle of a tempest; Partridge was in love with Carrington and Carrington with the homosexual Strachey, who adored Partridge, among others. Partridge wanted to marry Carrington and sought advice on how to go about it. Leonard suggested that he "put a pistol" to her head (Lee, 457). Apparently, Partridge took the advice, and he and Carrington were disastrously wed, but all of the emotional baggage surrounding the incident and its participants put a strain on relations with Strachey as well as the members of the Press. Leonard felt that Partridge was so overcome that he was failing to do his job; Partridge felt that Leonard was bossy, domineering, and too meticulous. By the autumn of 1922, Partridge was asked to leave.

In the summer of 1921, Virginia was ill with depression, as were both T.S. Eliot and his wife, Vivien. She began to think about suicide. She recovered enough to finish *Jacob's Room* by November. She decided to take a break from it before revising and fell sick. The beginning of 1922 was spent recovering from influenza, working on translations with S.S. Koteliansky, and attempting a story called "Mrs. Dalloway on Bond Street." Virginia felt shaky and abused. Published in March, *Monday or Tuesday* had been ignored by *The Times*; later reviews were negative. Her illness had progressed, the symptoms so severe the doctors falsely diagnosed her with lung disease, one of whom assured her that the bacteria causing it were embedded in her teeth. As a result, she had three teeth pointlessly removed. She would use her fury and disillusionment with these doctors, as well as those from her past, to create the doctors of Septimus Smith in *Mrs. Dalloway* (Leaska, 219).

Late spring found her revising *Jacob's Room* and hatching an ill-advised philanthropic scheme with Ottoline Morrell. The two had decided that T.S. Eliot should no longer work at Lloyd's, the English bank; this portion of the plan Eliot whole-heartedly agreed with. They decided that there might be a way by which they could raise enough money among friends, intellectuals and lovers of literature to support Eliot so that he might write. They called the plan the Eliot Fellowship. They spent mornings "writing letters, distributing circulars, and soliciting friends (and strangers)" (Leaska, 219). Not surprisingly, the plan failed utterly, never even raising one hundred pounds, much less the five hundred pounds that Eliot felt was the lowest sum upon which he might retire. The writers and other artists they approached were having enough trouble keeping food on their own tables to patronize the competition. Five years would pass before Ottoline and Virginia finally returned what little money they had gathered to Eliot's patrons.

When she wasn't worried about the future of Eliot, she was worried about her own. *Jacob's Room* mined new territory and sought different ways in which to communicate experience. Virginia began to worry that the work would be dismissed and she would be named mad. She began looking for ways to distract herself. There was the pleasure of Proust, a new discovery, and the mean pleasure she took in denouncing *Ulysses* in her diary. She wrote, "Never did I read such tosh [—] ... merely the scratching of pimples on the body of the bootboy at Claridges" (Leaska, 220). Still, the distractions were not enough; it was the praise of Leonard and an effusive letter from her American publisher, Brace, that fortified her. When *Jacob's Room* came out on October 27, reactions, again, were mixed. Some critics felt utterly lost; Arnold Bennett, a novelist, accused Virginia of writing characters who "did not vitally survive in the mind": he thought her novel mere stylings (Lee, 450). The *TLS* review disagreed, citing Jacob Flanders, the 'silent young man,' as one whose characterization was enhanced by the novel's technique. But it was Bennett who would remain with her, and to Bennett she further explained her style and technique, and its direct opposition to his, in *Mr. Bennett and Mrs. Brown*.

In addition to accolades, the winter of 1922 brought Virginia into contact with the most passionate, romantic love of her life, Vita Sackville-West—a novelist, a renowned lesbian dilettante, an aristocrat from one of England's most distinguished houses, and a vivid social presence. Though initially put off by her larger-than-life persona, Virginia swapped books with her and attended a few dinners, but Vita's impact did not truly come until later in the year. 1923 began with the death of Katherine Mansfield, a blow to Virginia, and the development of a correspondence with Jacques Raverat, a French painter. Raverat served as a literary critic for her, and close friend, perhaps because his was an art form different from that of the intensely rivalrous Virginia. She was also working on a book of critical essays, *The Common Reader*, and the manuscript which would become *Mrs. Dalloway*, "The Hours."

As she toiled, the months passed, and the beginning of 1924 brought a great boon to Hogarth Press. Leonard had successfully negotiated for the publication and distribution rights for the papers of the International Psycho-analytic Library, thereby securing publication of the first two volumes of Freud's *Collected Papers* to be published in English. It also brought a change of address. Hogarth Press and the Woolfs moved to 52 Tavistock Square, back into the city that Virginia had so missed during her time at Monk's House. In the midst of the chaos of moving in, Virginia invited Vita to lunch early in March. She suggested during that lunch that Vita might write something for the Press. Vita agreed; it was an opportunity of both the head and the heart. Notorious for falling quickly and completely in love, Vita became obsessed with a feeling that Virginia was soon to return. She invited Virginia to her ancestral home, Knole, a 365-room estate that had been given to the family by Queen Elizabeth I in 1566. Both Vita and her home became fodder; Virginia made them into celebrities in England with *Orlando*, a book-cum-love letter, written about and for Vita. A few days later, Vita left for vacation, and Virginia was left to stew about this intriguing woman. When Vita returned in September, she brought a manuscript, *Seducers in Equador*, and it was dedicated to Virginia.

In spite of her growing fascination with Vita, or perhaps because of it, Virginia turned to her work, deciding that she would repudiate all of Bennett's objections to *Jacob's Room* by explaining the virtues of her method of fiction, and the detriments of his. She also conceived of a new book, one she developed while revising *The Common Reader* and *Mrs. Dalloway*. The idea had come from a memory of her father, and she began writing it on May 14, 1925, a month after the publication of *The Common Reader*, which brought her accolades from the *TLS* and *The Manchester Guardian*. As was generally the case with her novels, *Mrs. Dalloway* had mixed reviews, but Virginia felt triumphant. Her American publisher had accepted both books with a royalty payment of 15%; a German publisher wanted to buy the rights to her books; an agent was heading over from America to meet with her, and the proceeds were enough to make improvements to Monk's House. In her glory, Virginia socialized, meeting and greeting throughout the summer, only to faint in August at the birthday party of her nephew Quentin. Leonard brought her back to Monk's House for a needed break, but her mania may not have solely been brought on by social commitments. Between August 6 and August 19, she had penned 22 pages of *To the Lighthouse*, and in so doing, raised all her family ghosts. She re-imagined the summers the Stephen family had spent together at Talland House, bringing her mother and her sister Stella back to life in Mrs. Ramsay, her querulous father back as Mr. Ramsay, and herself as Cam. Thoby, Adrian, Vanessa and even the servants appeared in the book, and Virginia was getting to tell the story in her own style, one that gave primacy to the emotional resonance of the moment, as well as the incidentals of circumstance.

FALLING IN LOVE

By October 2, the Woolfs had returned to London, but Virginia was still not well. Lytton Strachey's niece, Dr. Elinor Rendel, came to look at Virginia; Rendel would become her doctor for the rest of her life. She advised rest, and Virginia took it for October and November, but she was also thinking of Vita, worrying that they would be split apart by the assignment of Vita's husband, Harold Nicolson, to Tehran for two years. Nicolson was perfectly aware of his wife's interest in other women; he was interested in other men. Both had affairs, but both retained a peculiar allegiance to their own marriage of companionship and friendship. Much of what is known about Vita's response to Virginia and their relationship is gathered from letters that Vita sent to her husband. By December, Virginia was sufficiently healed for an outing with Vita, an invitation to her home, Long Barn, where they spent three nights together. In a letter to Harold, Vita claims to have slept with Virginia for the first time during this visit. Virginia was madly in love and begging for affection.

　　The letters that passed between the two women during Vita's two months in Tehran during the beginning of 1926 clearly illustrate the taking up of roles. Virginia wrote as the naïve, virginal lover, made weak with desire, necessitating the constant love, support, and approval of the older, more worldly, more masculine, sexual, arrogant, maternal woman. As Leaska points out repeatedly in his biography of Woolf, *Granite and*

Rainbow, the roles in this relationship mirrored those of Leslie and Julia, with Virginia enacting the pleas for sympathy that she had so despised in her father. Still, Virginia couldn't quite quell the critic inside; she studied Vita, writing to her, "And isn't there something that doesn't vibrate in you: It may be purposely—you don't let it: but I see it with other people, as well as with me: something reserved, muted—God knows what.... It's in your writing too.... The thing I call central transparency—sometimes fails you there too" (Leaska, 257). Vita agreed with the diagnosis, and it put her ill at ease. It was looking a little too deeply into who she was; the rigid roles of the letters were a little more comfortable, and she tried to reinstate them in the letters that followed.

At the same time that Virginia was imitating her father in life, she was recreating him in art. She raced through *To the Lighthouse*, finishing the first part in mid-April with reminders of her father cropping up everywhere. She visited novelist Thomas Hardy on July 25; her father had been the first to encourage Hardy as a young writer. The pace of the book and the reminder of her parents left her tired and depressed; she returned to Monk's House to rest and to write. She finished her novel in September, having split time on it with a short lesbian-interest story called "Slaters Pins Have No Points." When she returned to London, she finished revising the novel, all the while thinking of Vita and making time to see her and write to her. Vita was leaving for Persia in January 1927; Vanessa, Virginia's other support, was in the south of France with Duncan; and Virginia felt alone and ready for a change. She had her hair cut short, 'shingled', and she was so pleased with the result that she wrote of it to both Vita and Vanessa, feeling herself a whole new woman. This little vanity was typical of Virginia; she was terrified of being laughed at, and obsessed with people's reactions to her. A handsome haircut pleased her immensely, particularly as she felt herself attacked on other fronts. Her sister, Vanessa, had been reading Virginia's letters aloud to Duncan Grant and Clive. Clive took it upon himself to make fun of Virginia and her letters to a series of people. Virginia was furious with Clive, but she felt betrayed by Vanessa. A rift was widening between them based on this; Vanessa's obsessive love of her children from which Virginia felt excluded; and Virginia's monetary success. Virginia was making a good deal of money with her art, while Vanessa was making little. Virginia's attempt to soothe Vanessa was to play the martyr and remind her sister that she had children, while suffering

Virginia did not. In Virginia's mind, it seemed a fair exchange. To Vanessa, it must have seemed a slap in the face.

To the Lighthouse, published in May, brought the sisters a little closer. It was dedicated to Roger Fry, in thanks for his support and encouragement, but it was to Vanessa that she looked for the kind of criticism no one else could offer. She wanted to know if it was true to their parents. Vanessa responded in a heartfelt letter:

> It seemed to me in the first part of the book you have given me a portrait of mother which is more like her to me than anything I could ever have conceived possible. It is almost painful to have her so raised from the dead. You have made one feel the extraordinary beauty of her character, which must be the most difficult thing in the world to do.... You have given father too I think as clearly.... So you see as far as portrait painting goes you seem to me to be a supreme artist and it is so shattering to find oneself face to face with these two again that I can hardly consider anything else (Lee, 473–474).

The responses from the critical press were also positive, and the book sold over 3,000 copies by July, enough so that Virginia could afford to buy a car. Leonard learned to drive quickly, but Virginia, who was not particularly coordinated outside the realm of bowls, hit a child as she was driving. Apparently the collision was 'gentle' and the child was unhurt, but Virginia decided to leave the driving to Leonard, who was more adept.

In the midst of her professional accolades, Virginia was suffering personally. Vita had begun a new affair, one that would satisfy her physically, as apparently Virginia was unable. By July, Virginia realized that Vita's attention was gone, and she decided to entice her errant lover back with charms that the new woman couldn't hope to match: her intellect and her writing. She decided to write the fascinating Vita back into her life as the character of Orlando, who lives through five hundred years and one sex change. Vita became both man and woman for Virginia, with the sundry attractions of both. Through the summer and the early fall, Virginia let the idea gestate. She began her novel in October and finished it in March 1928—breakneck speed.

The novel was interrupted by a request from Bruce Richmond of *TLS*: Thomas Hardy had died on January 11; would she write an article on him? The article appeared on January 19, anonymously. Later that month, Vita's father died, leaving Knole to a male cousin rather than his daughter. Vita mourned for the loss of her family home, and Virginia continued writing the estate into her novel. When she finished working in March, she was tired, headachy, and ready for a break. She and Leonard decided to visit Vanessa and Duncan in Provence. The rest was restorative, and Virginia returned ready to revise the novel. The summer proved a time of positive press for Virginia. She received the *Femina Vie Heureuse* Prize on May 2, presented by her friend, the novelist Hugh Walpole; she met one of the best hostesses in London, Sibyl Colefax, and Virginia was thinking more about Vita, the possibility of losing her, and the publication of *Orlando*. During the summer, she and Vita had talked of going away together to Burgundy; Virginia saw this as a last chance to be with her, and she took it, in spite of her concerns about Leonard's response and her growing concern that it might cause her and Vita to fall out of love, once all of their secrets were revealed. They left on September 24. That morning, Virginia had quarreled with Leonard about the trip. Worried, she spent most of the week writing to Leonard and waiting desperately for a reply. Eventually she received a reply and calmed, but the romantic sojourn so sweetly imagined was not to be. It bore a much more marked resemblance to a maternal friendship, similar to the one with Violet Dickinson, though spiced with talk of literature, men and women.

The publication of *Orlando* in October brought Virginia a few more flattering letters from Vita, who wrote that she was 'dazzled, bewitched, enchanted' (Lee, 512). Vita's mother, on the other hand, known for her meddling and numerous court appearances for non-payment to various household workers, reviled the book. Next to the author photograph in the book, she wrote, "The awful face of a mad woman whose successful mad desire is to separate people who care for each other. I loathe this woman for having changed my Vita and taken her away from me" (Lee, 513). Never one to suppress any emotion, she sent Virginia a nasty letter, as well. The public, however, embraced the novel. Within six months, English sales were at 6,000 copies and the American sales topped 13,000. Woolf was a bona fide success story. October was a month of another sort of triumph: Virginia Woolf, self-educated in her father's library, denied education due to her sex, was asked to give two lectures at Cambridge University. The papers that she delivered, "Women and Fiction" became *A Room of One's Own*, the now famous feminist treatise.

A PUBLIC IDENTITY

In the midst of all of the upheaval, Virginia co-wrote a letter of protest with E.M. Forster, with whom she had become friends in 1910. Radclyffe Hall had written a novel, *The Well of Loneliness*, describing a lesbian love. The press was outraged, and under pressure from the government, the publisher, Jonathan Cape, had withdrawn the book. Now the Woolfs and Forster were outraged. The censorship went against their idea of the freedom of the press; Virginia and Forster penned a letter of protest which appeared in both *Nation and Athenaeum*. A host of fellow writers were prepared to testify, George Bernard Shaw among them. The publisher was asked to show proof as to why the book was not obscene and not worthy of immediate destruction. When it came to the Chief Magistrate, he accepted no claims of literary merit, summarily declared it obscene, dismissed all appeals, and ordered the book destroyed. Though Virginia was disgusted at the verdict, she was also disgusted by the book; she referred to it as "Well of all that's stagnant and lukewarm" (Leaska, 279). Nonetheless, she believed fervently in freedom of the press, as it was exactly that freedom which had allowed her to write as she pleased, regardless of gender or style.

The new year 1929 began poorly with an ill-advised trip to Berlin, where Virginia was made painfully aware that Vita no longer held a tendre for her. They had a private lunch in the midst of the larger party of Clive, Vanessa, Duncan, Leonard, and Harold Nicolson. At the lunch, Virginia spoke passionately of her love for Vita, only to be met with a lukewarm response. The great love affair of Virginia's life was over, or rather, it was over for Vita. Virginia persisted in whining, cajoling, manipulating, bullying, and begging Vita to love her for the remainder of her life. When they returned from Berlin, Virginia became ill; she had to be nearly carried from the ship, and heavily assisted by Leonard onto the train. She spent two weeks recovering. When she came out of it, she turned to her traditional solace, writing. In her mind, she had been fermenting *The Waves* and resolutely revising *Room*. In February, she decided to build herself a bedroom and a studio, rooms of her own, a decision that echoed her book. The Press was working on a uniform edition of her work, and by May, she was devising a plan for the novel. Before she began it in earnest, she and Leonard took a vacation in Cassis to see Vanessa, Duncan, and Julian, her nephew.

Over the past few years, Virginia had kept up a lively correspondence with both of her nephews. With Quentin, the letters were full of teasing and banter. He wanted to be a painter, and Virginia encouraged him. With Julian, relations were different, strained for a number of reasons, most of which boil down to jealousy. Julian was, always had been, and would continue to be the most important person in his mother's life. The two were, Virginia noted, 'in love' with each other; such a love excluded Virginia, displaced her from Vanessa's affection. In addition, Julian fancied himself a writer, clearly infringing on Virginia's territory. She was the writer of the family; it was the one thing that made up for the fact that she did not have children, that she was not sexual and free, that she was not Vanessa. She wanted no one to horn in on her territory. Julian, in his own way, was equally contentious, critical of the Bloomsbury Group, devoted to all things masculine in a way that disgusted Virginia, and in love with Joyce and the idea of self in writing. Even his aesthetic judgments seemed in opposition to hers. If they steered clear of writing, war, and Vanessa, the relationship remained largely civil, but when those taboo topics came up, Virginia bristled and Julian replied in the like. With Vanessa, Virginia needed to avoid talk of motherhood, fame, and money. These dual tensions made the trip to Cassis occasionally uneasy.

On June 23, she saw the opening of *The Waves*: "I think it will begin like this: dawn; the shells on a beach ... then all the children at a long table—lessons ... [T]his shall be childhood[,] ... the sense of children; unreality.... [t]here must be great freedom from 'reality'" (Lee 295). Though she had seen the beginning of the novel, she saw little else, and the writing went slowly, drawn through a series of style censors. She wanted the emotion of the moment without the overt explanation of traditional novels. It was to accumulate emotions, images, rather than facts; meaning would not be deduced; it would be *induced*. By July, Virginia was down with a headache, brought on partly by the writing and partly by the new woman in Vita's life. Without Vanessa, without

Vita, she was feeling intensely lonely and depressed. She lashed out at Vita in letters, demanding her affection and explanations for every moment spent away from her. In August, she had another round of headaches, which she paraded to Vita as evidence of what her desertion had done. It was a Leslie Stephen-like response.

October brought some relief as *A Room of One's Own* was met with nearly unanimous applause. Vita even reviewed it positively in her BBC radio show. Though Virginia was pleased, she was staggering through her novel, every step plodding and painful. This was not the easy writing of *Orlando*. It was a labor to put together something completely new and an elegiac attempt to remember the old: Thoby.

OUT WITH THE NEW, IN WITH THE OLD

Virginia concentrated on *The Waves* during 1930; she wrote, mentally battling the intricacies of form and the ways in which she might sustain them. When she was not writing she was socializing, seeing the opera, meeting old friends and new. In February, she saw George Duckworth again, who reminded them both of his status (knighted) and other narcissistic pleasures and accomplishments. Lytton Strachey came for tea, telling absorbing stories about Christopher Columbus; and Virginia met "a bluff military old woman," Ethel Smyth (Bishop 128). Smyth, an ardent feminist, had read *A Room of One's Own* and sent an admiring letter to Virginia. Virginia, always eager for affirmation and adulation, agreed to meet Smyth. She was charmed at the raging energy of the 72-year-old, a woman who was a composer, an ex-con, a suffragette, and an autobiographer. She was brash, arrogant, demanding, and not as smart as Virginia. The two trundled along, gladdened by each other for a time, but that changed as Virginia became more stressed. Despite the new friendship, *The Waves* obsessed her. She began the year using a vision she remembered from 1926, a distant fin in deep waters. It translated directly into Percival's death. She continued to write, reconsidering her formal options continuously, so much so that the normal letdown on completing the novel didn't creep up on her. The form held her enthralled through the book's end, but it also exhausted her. After the careful concentration of the summer, she collapsed as she was rewriting the book in August. She did not return to London until October.

In November, one of her infamous troubles was given notice: the bossy, wheedling, complaining Nelly Boxall. Boxall had come as a servant to the Woolfs early in their married life. She became in some way bonded to the couple, particularly Virginia, but the relationship was always tempestuous. Boxall complained about her mistress, her wages, her duties, but refused to leave when given notice. This caused Virginia a great deal of stress, and Boxall stayed on another three months before Virginia succeeded in officially firing her. Perhaps because of that stress, or the stress of the writing, Virginia caught influenza in December and remained bedridden—though mentally she was at work, piecing together *The Waves* in imagined revisions. By January, she was writing again, but her focus was so intense that she could only work for an hour at a time. When she finally finished her draft in February, she wrote in her diary, "I wrote the words O Death fifteen minutes ago, having reeled across the last ten pages with some moments of such intensity and intoxication that I seemed to stumble after my own voice ... (as when I was mad). I was almost afraid, remembering the voices that used to fly ahead. Anyhow it is done; and I have been sitting these 15 minutes in a state of glory, and calm, and some tears, thinking of Thoby.... Whether good or bad, it's done" (Leaska 308–309). The book had allowed Virginia to reconcile Thoby's death, to write him into a complete life, not the abruptly shortened one he'd had. The rivalry with Vanessa over Thoby was finished, as well. She owned him now as her sister never could.

Surprisingly, in the midst of all the intensity, Virginia brainstormed a new book that January, one that would conclude what she had begun with *A Room of One's Own*. It was to address women's sexual lives, and it became *The Years* (originally titled *The Pargiters*). She put *The Waves* aside for the time being and concentrated on socializing, a bad idea after the exhaustion and excitement of the book; she found herself rocked in large parties, panicked and unable to cope with her surroundings. She also battled the desperate feeling she had every time she finished a book. Leonard decided that they needed a short vacation, and the pair toured France for three weeks, after attending the strangely saddening funeral of her nemesis, Arnold Bennett. When she returned from vacation, she set a schedule for revision of the book.

Her plan was soon ruined by a marauding Ethel Smyth, enraged by a conductor's refusal to stage her opera. Smyth came to Virginia in a rage that lasted hours, was accompanied by documents, and was punctuated by Smyth's demands: "'You've got to listen to me—You've got to listen,' she kept saying and indeed the whole of 52 rang with her vociferations" (Leaska 311). Virginia finally had to shout that she had a headache to get Smyth to quiet and leave. Little more than a week later, Virginia was laid low by headaches and flashing lights in her eyes. Her diary mentions her constant thoughts of suicide, quelled only by Leonard. Her relationship with Ethel was further strained when Ethel asked Virginia to look at her latest section of her autobiography, *Female Pipings in Eden*. Virginia agreed, but her more-than-candid criticism did not sit well with Smyth, who felt herself abused. A series of mollifying letters were exchanged before the friendship could continue.

Despite the trouble with Ethel, Virginia finished the book on July 17, a month later than scheduled. Attacked with her usual nerves, she gave the manuscript to Leonard, who read it carefully, and declared it "a masterpiece." Virginia was ecstatic. When they returned for the summer at Rodmell in late July, she decided that she needed to write something light, with which she might relax a little, and she hatched the idea for *Flush* a week later. *Flush* was a biography of sorts, told from the perspective of Elizabeth Barrett Browning's cocker spaniel. She alternated between corrected proofs and her little diversion. Unfortunately, the diversion was not enough to keep her from obsessing over the release of *The Waves*, scheduled for October. The first week of September, she rested, trying to recover from a series of incapacitating headaches. Press apprentice John Lehmann helped relieve her fears a little when he sent word that he "loved" the book. Friends wrote to congratulate her, but the popular media was once again confused and fragmented in their reactions.

Virginia pressed on, turning again to her longtime solace: work. She began a second collection of literary essays that became the second *Common Reader*. She also worked on a piece called *Letter to a Young Poet*, dedicated to John Lehmann and his friends Stephen Spender, W.H. Auden, C. Day Lewis, and Christopher Isherwood. She was ill briefly in November, but the year was most remembered for the illness and death of her dear friend Lytton Strachey.

In mid-December, Dora Carrington wrote of Strachey's illness. Virginia called for daily updates, but there was little to say. He died on January 21, 1932. Both of the Woolfs grieved his loss bitterly and worried over the distraught Carrington. On March 10, they visited her at Strachey's home. Carrington was distressed, either on the verge of tears or sobbing. As they were leaving Carrington gave Virginia a small French box that she, Carrington, had given to Strachey. The next day Carrington committed suicide by placing a gun between her thighs and firing. It took her six hours of agony before she died. Virginia wrote it all into her diary in a mixture of mourning and reportage.

LITERARY LEGACY

Virginia was a literary success, but her old friends were dying and she was getting older. She was asked to give the Clark Lectures in Literature at Cambridge, a series whose first speaker had been her father. Virginia was the first woman to be asked, but she had little time, with three books brewing, and she turned down the offer. Still, it was gratifying to be asked, a girl who was not formally educated speaking at one of the foremost institutions of learning. She was thrilled both for herself and for her father; she had followed in his footsteps. She was also receiving press from friends. Hugh Walpole dedicated *The Waverley Pageant* to Virginia; three books about her were published; early in 1933, Manchester University offered her an honorary doctorate, which she refused.

The year started out with tension. John Lehmann, who had come to the Press with the idea of serving as an apprentice and then a partner, was frustrated. He wanted the Press to be a place for the younger poets, and Leonard disagreed. Their quarreling eventually lead to Lehmann leaving in September. Virginia did not help matters when she published *Letter to a Young Poet*, in which she took the younger poets to task for being too interested in the differences between people rather than the commonalities. She used quotes to emphasize her point, but apparently did not think enough of the poets to offer proper citation for the excerpts. The young men felt attacked.

To relax, Virginia and Leonard decided to take a small vacation in April with Roger Fry and his sister. The foursome went to Greece, where Virginia found herself liking Fry all over again, for his energy, his *joie de vivre*, his knowledge. When she returned to London, her vacation glow was short-lived. The up-and-coming critic M.C. Bradbrook criticized Virginia's writing, claiming that Virginia used rhetorical padding to avoid saying things which were truly harsh. By late May, she had fallen into depression, which included fainting spells and headaches. She finished the second *Common Reader* with little enthusiasm and spent the summer resting. Her episodes repeated in October, and by November, the doctors had prescribed digitalis and rest. But Virginia did not want rest; she needed work to sustain her, to see her through the publication of *Common Reader*. She awaited criticism as if awaiting a death sentence. The Press published her book on the same day as Vita's wildly successful novel *Family History*. Though it meant a financial boon for the Press, Virginia was enraged and jealous, writing nasty letters to Vita then repenting when she had calmed down. She turned to *The Years* to calm herself.

She had conceived of the novel while in the bath in 1930, preparing to give a paper before the National Society for Women's Service. When she actually began it in October 1932, she planned it as a novel-essay, alternating forms by chapter. She wanted to discuss women's roles and sexual lives. She had worked steadily through Christmas of 1932 but was worn out by April. Her heart beat irregularly, and she was exhausted. She used May to relax and continued working through the summer. The writing felt laborious, and she had to break it up with revising *Flush*, which she no longer liked. Without Lytton as her audience, the joke felt stale. Still, she finished it in August, and it became the October selection of the American Book Society.

In addition to her troubles with the book, she suffered another setback; Vita was in love with Gwen St. Aubyn, her sister-in law, and the two were living together in Sissinghurst, leaving Virginia feeling excluded and unloved. She felt Vanessa slipping further away, as well. Julian's dissertation had been denied by King's College, and Vanessa was having financial difficulties. In an attempt to help her sister, Virginia bought her a car for her birthday, claiming that it was a dual present, for Duncan as well. But the gesture of largesse just emphasized the financial gap between them and pushed Vanessa further from her. As Vanessa was drifting, so were less loved members of the family. On holiday in Ireland, the Woolfs happened to see a death announcement in the April 27, 1934 newspaper: George Duckworth was dead. Virginia's feelings were mixed, but largely nostalgic for the childhood memories she had of George, somehow excepting the abuse.

To ease the pain of estrangement, Virginia turned to her work, trying desperately to reconcile the facts of her essay with the truth of her story. Eventually, she decided that the two could not be made to fit together. She put the essays aside and attacked the narrative portion anew. The grand experiment had not worked. By September, she was flushed and tense, the writing was not going well, and her nephew Julian had decided to head to China and distress his mother. (Denied fellowship twice at Cambridge, he had applied to the National University of Wuhan in China.) Vanessa was dismayed, and in her obsession with her son, more distant still from her agitated sister. The agitation continued with the death of Roger Fry, a man who had fulfilled the father role in Virginia's life. He had encouraged her in her writing and her personal life. It was a stunning blow, but one that energized her writing. She finished her first draft of *The Years* on September 30. The following day she developed headaches. The *TLS* advertised Wyndham Lewis's book *Men Without Art*, which devoted an entire chapter to deriding Virginia. With the end of her novel, and the nasty press, she was seriously depressed by mid-October.

She spent the next several months revising *The Years*, and reading an increasing number of writers criticizing both her and Bloomsbury. Virginia did her own criticizing, being perhaps overly candid with Julian when he sent poems to the Press. It did nothing to bridge the distance between her and Vanessa. Frustrated, suffering from headaches, the Woolfs again decided to take a vacation, one of the most ill-conceived trips they would ever take.

They decided to drive through Germany down to Austria, completely aware that the Nazi Party was gathering unbelievable strength and numbers. Undaunted by the warnings of the Foreign Office, they secured a letter of passage from Prince Otto van Bismarck and proceeded on their way. Not only was Leonard Jewish, but the pair were both well-known for their political views, which were completely antithetical to those of the Nazis. Still, they plunged into the whole thing with great verve, taking with them their pet marmoset, Mitz. Throughout the drive, they encountered Nazi propaganda in every town. As they reached Bonn, a German policeman tried to wave them back; the street was closed; Hermann Wilhelm Göring, president of the Reichstag, was en route. Before them, hundreds of people waved flags, from schoolkids to soldiers. Still, the intrepid pair drove through it all, with the top down. Luckily, the German people were utterly enamored of Mitz the marmoset, who perched atop Leonard's shoulder throughout the drive. Apparently, she was popular enough to divert all attention from the suspicious English couple.

Though the break was a welcome one, Virginia found herself ready to resume work on her manuscript, but when they returned it was to the news that their beloved dog, Pinka, had died. Virginia's mental state was slipping, and she became paranoid that critics were laughing at her, thinking her crazy. She sank into depression, and in the midst of it, Julian left for China, to be gone for three years. Virginia kept up a correspondence with her nephew but devoted much of that summer to revising and typing her draft. She broke up the writing by speaking at the memorial exhibit for Roger Fry on July 12. She was tense by September and ready for a break. Roger Fry's family had asked Virginia to write his biography; it was the break she needed. She planned to spend mornings on *The Years* and afternoons on Fry. But more pressure was still to come.

The Years had taken too long. Virginia had brought in little money in 1934–1935, and it was beginning to affect their finances. The pressure to finish was increasing, and around her, the nation was talking of Hitler and the possibility of war. On March 7, 1936, Hitler's troops marched into the Rhineland. Leonard and Virginia were members of the group For Intellectual Liberty, an assemblage with which Leonard became deeply involved. While Leonard was distracted, Virginia had mood swings, headaches, insomnia. When he realized what was happening, he took her to Monk's House to rest and postponed the publication of the book until 1937. This was the worst she had been in some time, spending all of April resting. Recovery was slow, and Leonard allowed her to revise for only an hour a day. The rest were to be spent recuperating. By November, she was mostly well, except for her fever over the book. She didn't like it; she felt it weak, incoherent. She feared that it would read as the ravings of a madwoman. Leonard read it carefully and told her it was "extraordinarily good" (Leaska, 376). Virginia recorded the moment in her diary: "Leonard put down the last sheet at about 12 last night and could not speak. He was in tears" (Leaska 376). Despite all of her fears about the failures of the book, Leonard liked it, and his approval relieved her of a great deal of her paranoia. Nevertheless, her initial judgment was not wholly wrong. Leonard later wrote in his autobiography that his response was incomplete. He thought the book too long, among other things, but wanted to reassure her due to her illness. It was enough to get her through the revisions. She sent the final pages to the printer at the end of December.

December brought other bittersweet happenings as well. Violet Dickinson, her fast friend from so many years ago, sent her an edition of all of her (Virginia's) letters bound together. She was given other reminders of old friends, as well. Her beloved Greek teacher, Janet Case, was dying. In fact, death seemed too present. Leonard became ill, and the doctors suggested prostate trouble, liver disease, a host of terrifying options, before giving him a clean bill of health. All of the trouble was sobering for Virginia. Without Leonard, there would be little reason to live. Again, for relief, Virginia turned to writing.

She had taken the essays originally meant to be a part of *The Years* and begun to work on them again. It was a distraction both from Leonard's health and the pending March 15 publication of her novel. When it finally came out, the *TLS* review was favorable, and though she was pleased not to have negative press, the review also posed a problem. If this book was being praised as much as other, better books, then perhaps her audience was lacking in discernment. Perhaps she had never been good and the foundation on which she had set herself was utterly false. Later reviews were highly critical, and though she felt brutalized, she also felt validated. Her opinion had been right, and her faith in her audience was restored. Still, stress was coming in from new arenas: this time it was a nephew.

Julian had written to Vanessa to tell her that he was resigning his post at Wuhan University to fight fascists in the Spanish Civil War. Vanessa begged her son to come home before leaving for Spain. He agreed, and came home for what was to be his last visit in June 1937. Both his aunt Virginia and his mother felt almost certain this was to be the last of him they would ever see. He left for Spain in early June, to be an ambulance driver. He was killed on July 18, three days after the death of Janet Case. Vanessa was in a tailspin. Her beloved child had died, and she was devastated beyond recovery. Leonard and Virginia took Vanessa to Charleston Farm and stayed themselves at Monk's House, a mere four miles away, close enough that the sisters could see each other everyday. Virginia did her best to soothe Vanessa and re-enter her affections. It was support that Vanessa desperately needed, support that it was probably healthful for Virginia to give. She saw Vanessa every day through August and September.

By October, she had finished the first draft of *Three Guineas*; revisions were completed in January 1938. In that same month, Virginia finally turned over her portion of the Press to John Lehmann. Originally, the plan had been for Lehmann, Spender, Auden, and Isherwood to buy the Press outright for six thousand pounds, with Lehmann donating three thousand of the six. Only Lehmann was able to secure his portion. Leonard then suggested that Lehmann buy out Virginia, and they signed an agreement in February, effective in April. Virginia was both relieved and a little nostalgic about the sale; it had become an influential enterprise, allowing both her and others a great deal of freedom, and it represented her partnership with Leonard.

March was full of other concerns, global concerns. Hitler had invaded Austria. The closer the war came, the more Virginia retreated into work and worried over the reception of *Three Guineas*. She began *Roger Fry* on April 1, 1938, and *Between the Acts* (originally called *Pointz Hall*) on April 2. *Three Guineas* was published in June, and immediately responses came pouring in. Virginia had denounced both wars and the men who fought in them. Friend and feminist Philippa "Pippa" Strachey, sister to Lytton, was delighted by the book; Vita was appalled. The popular press ranged from not particularly pleased to enraged. The atmosphere all over the country was tense with talk of war, and the book only exacerbated that talk in literary circles.

In political circles, Leonard was on the move. He and Virginia left for London, where he was needed in his capacity as Secretary of the Labour Party's Advisor's Committee. When they arrived, the entire city was preparing for war. Virginia spent the day going to the library to review letters for *Roger Fry*, and to the National Gallery. She watched and listened to people speaking of the inevitability of war, heard the government urging everyone who could to leave London as soon as possible. They prepared the Press, and left for Rodmell, where they took in two children and gathered supplies, steeling themselves for what was to come. Virginia used *Fry* as an escape, though the biography was causing trouble. She had to gloss over many of the facts of his love life, and she was desperate, again, to reconcile what she felt to be the truth of his life with the facts. The rest of year passed uneasily, with work and preparations for war.

When Virginia finally finished *Roger Fry* in March 1939, she had only a month's respite before world events would cause more hardship.

Hitler had invaded Czechoslovakia, and Mussolini had attacked Albania. As people tightened their financial belts, the Press hemorrhaged money. In London, the Press was surrounded by construction and demolition, inspiring the weary Woolfs to secure the lease on 37 Mecklenburgh Square, even though they could not rid themselves of the Tavistock lease. By June, despite a small vacation, Virginia was becoming depressed and tense from the revisions of the biography. September brought worse news still: Great Britain had declared war on Germany. England was to be bombed again. The Woolfs again retreated to Monk's House, where Virginia had to be content with letters from Ethel and from Vita, who was either entrenched at Sissinghurst or driving a local ambulance. Both filled Virginia with terror. Virginia worked on revising the biography, and in early February 1939, she finished it and gave the manuscript to friends and family, fraught, as she always was, with anxiety over their responses. While Vanessa and Fry's family were positive, Leonard was brutally critical. Virginia, now convinced of her failure, turned to *Pointz Hall (Between the Acts)* for solace and to a piece that she had begun writing at Vanessa's advice, her own autobiographical piece, "A Sketch of the Past."

In spite of the writing, there was little solace to be had as the country and Virginia with it, watched in horror as Hitler's machine increased in power and gall. The Nazis had invaded Holland, Luxembourg, and Belgium. Chamberlain had resigned, and her brother, Adrian, had secured lethal doses of morphine for Leonard and Virginia, who planned a suicide pact for when the Germans invaded England. Times were grim, and no amount of writing was going to change that. In fact, the war had rendered Virginia Woolf largely obsolete. There was little time to think about fiction when the story immediately before the population had such relevance. Though the press received *Fry* well, it was a fleeting acknowledgment, second- and third-shelf news at best. Even Virginia was distracted. Mecklenburgh Square was hit by the Germans in September, then the house itself was damaged a few days later. They moved the Press to Hertfordshire. Virginia tried to work, to conceive of something relevant. She came up with the idea for a common history book, but she was distracted by the loss of another house. Tavistock Square had been hit. Planes roared above them, in London, in Rodmell. Everywhere there was the distant and not-so-distant sound of fighting and explosions. The need for writers was gone. There was only need now for soldiers and survivors. Virginia was beginning to feel lost. She turned to writing to make herself present again.

The work on *Pointz Hall* was focused, furious, and draining. As pages accrued, the fear of death grew stronger and more omnipresent. In the autumn of 1940, the focus began to shift into mood swings, manic highs and desperate lows. By the end of November, she had completed a second draft of *Pointz Hall*. She turned to her social history, again writing furiously. The next few months, the last of her life, were filled with terror, despair, and exhaustion. Her writing hand now shook, a palsy brought on by overuse; she felt old. The war was raging, plunging them into darkness and threatening all those she loved. *Pointz Hall* still wasn't right after the third draft. There seemed little reason to live. In December, she read through her parents' love letters. She was powerfully reminded of their missing presence and her desire for them. At the New Year, she was profoundly depressed. On March 12, while walking with friend and doctor Octavia Wilberforce, Virginia told her that she was "feeling desperate—depressed to the lowest depths" (Leaska, 435). She seemed haunted by her father, speaking of his effects on the children, saying that he "threw himself too much on us. Made too great emotional claims ... and I think that has accounted for many of the wrong things in my life. I never remember any enjoyment of my body" (Leaska, 435). The ghost of her father, more than the Duckworth boys and their abuse, haunted her, fragmented her. Six days later, Virginia tried to kill herself, by drowning in the River Ouse. She drafted a suicide note and left it for Leonard. Apparently, he missed the note as he went out to meet her. It was raining, so when Virginia arrived, soaked to the bone and rattled, he suspected little. She claimed to have slipped and fallen into the river. Still, Leonard was uneasy, and he spoke with Vanessa about it.

Vanessa came the next day to see Virginia, to try to convince her to rest. When she returned home, she wrote what she intended to be a reassuring and reasonable letter, asking Virginia to rest—for what would they do if she became an invalid and England was invaded? Surely, this seed of terror could not have helped matters. Octavia came to visit again, and Virginia was distraught, claiming that she could not write, and without the writing, she could not handle the pain. A few days later, Virginia wrote a letter to John Lehmann regarding *Between the Acts*, belittling the book, calling it stupid and trivial. Leonard added a cover note explaining the situation. OctaviaWilberforce visited again, trying to persuade Virginia to rest, possibly to go to a private facility. Virginia responded plaintively, begging not be given the rest cure. The next day, March 28, 1941, after Leonard headed to the lodge, Virginia left suicide notes for Leonard and for Vanessa, put on her fur coat, took her walking stick, and left for the river. From her past experience, she knew to add stones to her pockets before entering into the river. When Leonard returned to the house, he read the letter and became frantic. He went to the river and found her walking stick floating in the water. Though policeman dived for hours, her body wasn't found until April 18.

At the beginning of April, the newspapers were filling with her disappearance and elegiac pieces written by friends. Leonard received over two hundred letters and responded to each. The papers published quotes from her suicide note, some incorrectly. Leonard was left to the painful task of correcting their mistakes. In the midst of his grief, he decided a plan of management with Lehmann. They would publish *Between the Acts*, and other papers, keeping Virginia a public figure for years to come. In fact, from the teens on, no decade of the 20th century was without a publication by Virginia Woolf.

WORKS CITED

Bell, Quentin. *Virginia Woolf: A Biography*. 2 vols. London: Hogarth Press, 1972.

Bishop, Edward. *A Virginia Woolf Chronology*. London: Macmillan Press, 1989.

Leaska, Mitchell. *Granite and Rainbow: The Hidden Life of Virginia Woolf*. New York: Farrar, Straus and Giroux, 1998.

Lee, Hermione. *Virginia Woolf*. New York: Alfred A. Knopf, 1997.

Stape, J.H., ed. *Virginia Woolf: Interviews and Recollections*. Iowa City: University of Iowa Press, 1995.

Woolf, Virginia. *Moments of Being*. ed. Jeanne Schulkind. 2nd ed. New York: Harcourt, Brace & Company, 1985.

NEIL HEIMS

Recomposing Reality: An Introduction to the Work of Virginia Woolf

Let us record the atoms
as they fall upon the mind in the order in which they fall, let us trace the
pattern, however disconnected and
incoherent in appearance, which
each sight or incident scores upon
consciousness.

—Virginia Woolf, "Modern Fiction"

MODERNISM

Perhaps more widely known for the appearance of her name in the title of Edward Albee's play about a dysfunctional academic family, or for the fictionalization of her persona on film by Nicole Kidman, than for her actual accomplishment, Virginia Woolf nevertheless is a writer whose work played a pivotal role in shaping the literature and the culture of the twentieth century. Beginning with *Jacob's Room* in 1923 and going through *Mrs. Dalloway* (1925), *To the Lighthouse* (1927), *Orlando* (1928), *The Waves* (1931), and *The Years* (1937), Woolf repeatedly redefined the scope and capacities of the novel and drew it further and further away from the characteristic form it had assumed in the nineteenth century. And *A Room of One's Own* (1929), Woolf's eloquent assault on the degraded position of women in society and literature, became one of the most influential texts of twentieth-century social criticism. Living from 1882 through 1941, Woolf saw and charted the transition of consciousness from Victorian confidence and Edwardian upheaval to Modernist perplexity and phenomenological relativism.[1]

The driving force behind Modernism was the conviction that the conventions which had ostensibly guided the Victorian and Edwardian past[2] were insufficient for exploring, explaining, and describing what actually occurs in our everyday lives, or what we actually experience, or how we experience it. In the essay "Modern Fiction," Woolf wrote, "Our quarrel ... is not with the classics." ("Modern Fiction," 208) She regarded novelists like Fielding, Sterne, Austen, the Brontës, and Dickens highly. From its narrative intonations to its literary gymnastics, for example, it is clear that Woolf is drawing, in *Orlando*, on resources similar to ones Laurence Sterne used in *Tristram Shandy*. Because, for example, writes Woolf at one point in *Orlando*, "the most ordinary conversation is often the most poetic, and the most poetic is precisely that which cannot be written down," in a most Shandian way she then leaves a block of blank space on the page—and when she resumes writing, she says, "After some more of this kind of talk." (254) She held George Eliot in particular esteem because of her singular ability "to reason out the motives of the mind" (Bernard, 21), which is one of the principle tasks of Woolf's fiction, too, and Eliot's Dorothea Brooke of *Middlemarch*, with her complex mix of desire, selflessness, and the stubborn integrity of Antigone, can be seen in many of Woolf's heroines.

Woolf's quarrel was with the sort of literature represented by the work of writers like H.G. Wells, Arnold Bennett, and John Galsworthy, Edwardian contemporaries, all three of whom she criticized because they "are materialists.... concerned not with the spirit but with the body ... [and] they write of unimportant things: they spend immense skill and immense industry making the trivial and the transitory appear the true and the enduring" ("Modern Fiction," 209, 210) She means, particularly by the term "materialist," that these writers focus all their attention on the outer, factual side of human experience, and as antidote, Woolf asserts the writer must

> [l]ook within and life, it seems, is very far from being "like this." Examine for a moment an ordinary mind on an ordinary day. The mind receives a myriad of impressions— trivial, fantastic, evanescent, or engraved with the sharpness of steel. From all sides they come, an incessant shower of

innumerable atoms; and as they fall, as they shape themselves into the life of Monday or Tuesday, the accent falls differently from the old; the moment of importance came not here but there; so that if a writer were a free man and not a slave, if he could write what he chose, not what he must, if he could base his work upon his own feeling and not upon convention, there would be no plot, no comedy, no tragedy, no love interest or catastrophe in the accepted style.... Life is not a series of gig lamps symmetrically arranged; but a luminous halo, a semi-transparent envelope surrounding us from the beginning of consciousness to the end. ("Modern Fiction," 212)

Woolf concludes with the rhetorical question, "Is it not the task of the novelist to convey this varying, this unknown and uncircumscribed spirit, whatever aberration or complexity it may display, with as little mixture of the alien and external as possible?" ("Modern Fiction", 212–213) And in a tribute to James Joyce she indirectly answers it:

Mr. Joyce ... is concerned at all costs to reveal the flickerings of that innermost flame which flashes its message through the brain, and in order to preserve it he disregards ... whatever to him seems adventitious, whether it be probability, or coherence or any other of the signposts which for generations have served to support the imagination of the reader when called upon to imagine what he can neither touch nor see. ("Modern Fiction" 214)

It is just these "flickerings of the innermost flame," or that flame's absence, that Woolf repeatedly set out to describe and chronicle in her fiction. Modernism, then, was a response to both the certainty and the evasiveness of the nineteenth century and to the breakdown of confidence in the conventions which gave the nineteenth century its power.

The practitioners of Modernism drew on the new scientific, philosophical, political, and psychological methods and conclusions which crowned the end of the nineteenth century. These discoveries and hypotheses arose partially as a continuation of the humanistic quest for knowledge (which was sometimes harnessed, in disregard for humanistic values, by the Industrial Revolution) and partially as a response to the failure of traditional assumptions about values, people, and society. The overriding achievement of colonialism and empire, after all, by the end of the nineteenth century, seemed to be the brutality of war; among the fruits of the Industrial Revolution—the great capitalist disposition of labor and production—were poverty, injustice, and materialism; the cornerstone of moral decorum—correctness and self-effacing discipline, together with obedience to the laws of propriety in feeling, thought, and behavior—resulted in repression and nervous diseases. The consequence to humanity was often seen to be a deformed spirit and a denatured body.

Distress at these results engendered both discontent with the system which seemed to be responsible for them and new approaches to ways of knowing and being which might repair old troubles and prevent their recurrence. Sociologists like Karl Marx, natural scientists like Charles Darwin, moral and aesthetic critics like Matthew Arnold and John Ruskin, and psychologists like Sigmund Freud (whose works in English translation were first published in England by Woolf and her husband by their press, the Hogarth Press) not only interpreted the assumptions which governed individual and social behavior and phenomena in the nineteenth century, but their essential methodologies relied on the power of individual observation and perception. Such observation and perception was a practice which had been familiar to painters, poets, and novelists since the Renaissance. Considering this, it seems inevitable that Marx in his examination of class should have appreciated Balzac, or that Freud in his formulation of the psychoanalytic map of human consciousness should have relied so heavily on literature, and that the novelists who followed frequently referred to the insights of Marx and Freud in the delineation and presentation of their characters.

Central to the Modernist break with the past in writers like Virginia Woolf, James Joyce, Marcel Proust, D.H. Lawrence, T.S. Eliot, or Gertrude Stein was not a revision of the concept of *what* constituted reality, but a new vision of *how* reality was constituted, perceived, and represented, and an altered attitude towards reality. Consequently, what had perhaps previously been ignored, been condemned, or gone unperceived, in the work of Modernists had to be examined, attended to, and reevaluated. "For the moderns," Woolf wrote in "Modern Fiction," "the point of interest lies very likely in the dark places of psychology[;] ... the emphasis is upon something hitherto ignored." In order to realize that, a new relation to perception had to be formulated, and a use of language different from what had been developed in writing had to be imagined. "[A]t once a different outline of form becomes necessary," Woolf wrote, "difficult for us to grasp, incomprehensible to our predecessors." ("Modern Fiction," 215, 216) The omniscient and therefore authoritative—if not authoritarian—author/narrator was replaced by the shifting perspectives of the characters' thought and experience as if beamed from within rather than delivered from outside them. The language of the novel became the language of perception and thought, rather than of description, exposition, and explanation.

The attitude of the novel also underwent a change because of a critical reevaluation of what Woolf saw as the rotted and bloated texture of nineteenth-century life and art:

> Love, birth, and death were all swaddled in a variety of fine phrases. The sexes drew further and further apart. No open conversation was tolerated. Evasions and concealments were sedulously practised on both sides. And just as the ivy and the evergreen rioted in the damp earth outside, so did the same fertility show itself within. The life of the average woman was a succession of childbirths. She married at nineteen and had fifteen or eighteen children by the time she was thirty; for twins abounded. Thus the British Empire came into existence; and thus—for there is no stopping damp; it gets into the inkpot as it gets into the woodwork— sentences swelled, adjectives multiplied, lyrics became epics, and little trifles that had been essays a column long were now encyclopedias in ten or twenty volumes. (Woolf, *Orlando*, 229–230)

It is essential to remember, however, that critical responses to the disgraced institutions of the nineteenth century, although they exploded at the century's end, were, nevertheless, not entirely new. The writers who redefined literature and cultural values in the first decades of the twentieth century followed in the tradition (even as they refashioned it) of a number of nineteenth-century writers who had presented critical visions of the customs and attitudes of the nineteenth century, among them Charlotte Brontë (in *Jane Eyre*), Thomas Carlyle (in *Sarter Resartus*), Charles Dickens (in *Dombey and Son*), George Eliot (in *Middlemarch* and *Felix Holt, the Radical*), George Meredith (in "Modern Love"), William Butler (in *The Way of All Flesh*), and William Morris (in *News from Nowhere*). It was not the matter that was especially new in Modernist literature—although there certainly were breaks with the past, especially in the matter of sexuality, sexual relations, and the relation of the sexes—but the manner.

The Modernist belief was not founded, therefore, on the assumption that reality had changed, but that the attitudes and tools of perceiving reality had, and that reality had broadened and deepened because more of its aspects were considered both worthy of attention and capable of being probed. Modernist writers, thus, did not find themselves in an artistic vacuum but in the enviable position of having a world behind them to review, redefine, and recompose and the contemporary discoveries in psychology, philosophy, and painting to use in that endeavor. Nor, despite their challenge to tradition, did they suffer isolation. Woolf, for example, was born into a highly literary and well-connected Victorian family and enjoyed the support of a number of writers, artists, and intellectuals in her youth, who were collectively known as the Bloomsbury Group.

LESLIE STEPHEN'S FAMILY AND THE BLOOMSBURY GROUP

Woolf's pedigree as a novelist was impeccable. Her father was Sir Leslie Stephen, author of *The History of English Thought in the Eighteenth Century* (1876 and 1881) and *The Science of Ethics* (1882), among many other works, including books on his own mountain climbing expeditions and on Unitarianism. He also edited several important English literary journals, including *The Cornhill Magazine* and *The Pall Mall Gazette*. He was a literary critic and the editor of the immense *Dictionary of National Biography*, for which he also wrote many of the entries. He counted Henry James, George Meredith, Matthew Arnold, Thomas Hardy, Robert Browning, Robert Louis Stevenson, Lord Tennyson, Charles Eliot Norton, and George Eliot among his friends, colleagues, and acquaintances. Some, like James, Hardy, and Browning, occasionally dined with his family or were guests at his summer house in St. Ives and were familiar figures to his children. Woolf describes meeting James on the street one day when she was twenty-five:

> Henry James fixed me with his staring blank eye—it is like a childs marble—and said "My dear Virginia, they tell me— they tell me—they tell me—that you as indeed being your fathers daughter nay your grandfathers grandchild—the descendant I may say of a century—of a century—of quill pens and ink—ink—ink pots, yes, yes, yes, they tell me— ahm m m —that you, that you *write* in short." This went on in the public street. (Lee, 217)

Woolf's father's first wife, Harriet Marian Thackeray, had been the daughter of the novelist William Makepeace Thackeray. Woolf's mother was Julia Jackson Duckworth Stephen. Julia Stephen spent much of her life, although not a professional nurse, at the sickbed of friends and family members, caring for them, and she, too, was a writer. She wrote "on the morality and work ethic of 'agnostic women' [praising it] and on the [then] current debate on domestic service." (Lee, 83) But her essays, save for one, "Notes from Sick Rooms," remained unpublished. Her children's stories were entirely for the home consumption of her own children. Unlike her daughter Virginia's, her sensibility regarding the place of women in society was rooted in an acceptance of the traditional Victorian definition of women's roles, and she opposed and campaigned against "Female Suffrage." (Lee, 83) The family of Julia Stephen's first husband, Herbert Duckworth, owned the publishing company Duckworth's, which published some of Woolf's early work, including her first two novels, *The Voyage Out*, in 1915, and *Night and Day*, in 1919. Woolf's elder sister was the painter and interior designer Vanessa Bell. Her brother Adrian became a psychiatrist. Her favorite brother, Thoby, died at the age of twenty-six, in 1906, of typhus contracted on a trip the four of them had taken to Greece.

After their father died in 1904—their mother had died in 1895— Virginia and Vanessa, along with their brothers, Thoby and Adrian, left the family home, with its dark and heavy Victorian furnishings, and moved to a brighter house at 46 Gordon Square in Bloomsbury. This

house became the center of intellectual and artistic activity, principally
through Thoby. A student at Cambridge, he met a circle of bright young
men and invited them home. Soon, along with Virginia and Vanessa, this
core group—consisting of Clive Bell, a painter who would become
Vanessa's husband; Lytton Strachey, who is said to have revived the art
of biography with *Eminent Victorians* (1918) and *Queen Victoria* (1921);
Saxon Sydney-Turner, a brilliant and enigmatic figure who spent his life
in the British Civil Service; and Leonard Woolf, novelist, biographer,
printer and future husband, in 1912, of Virginia—began meeting every
Thursday. Without a chaperone; dressed informally, even for dinner;
speaking freely about art, literature, culture, philosophy, politics, sex—
whatever the members felt like discussing—they soon became rather
widely known for bohemianism. Others—Roger Fry, a critic, painter and
organizer of art exhibitions; Duncan Grant, a painter who became
Vanessa's companion when she separated from Clive Bell, and John
Maynard Keynes, the economist—joined the group. W.B. Yeats, E.M.
Forster, and Bertrand Russell also frequently attended the Bloomsbury
gatherings. "Bloomsbury" set the climate in which Virginia Woolf came
of age and, along with the home life of her childhood, exerted a
profound formative influence on her work.

     Another important determinant of the kind of work she did and
the way she did it was her own recurring mental turmoil. She knew "the
dark places of psychology" at first hand. There were, of course, her
recurrent, debilitating attacks of an illness—which Leonard Woolf called
manic depression—which tormented her in mind and body all her life,
and which was sometimes accompanied by suicide attempts; but there
was also an ongoing confrontation with her own family history and her
own emotional entanglement in that history. To make this connection
between her life story and her literature is to argue not that there is a
direct cause-and-effect relationship between Woolf's experience and
her fiction, but that her fictions both in matter and in manner—her
plots, themes, recurring concerns—are precipitates of her experience,
substances derived from it. Woolf herself states unambiguously in
Orlando that "every secret of a writer's soul, every experience of his life,
every quality of his mind is written large in his works." (Woolf,
Orlando, 209)

Ambivalent Attachments

The dominant response Woolf had to her family seems to have been ambivalence. There is indeed a consistent pattern of ambiguity in the characters of the important people around her, in their relation to her, and in her feelings about them. She had what one of her biographers, Hermione Lee, calls a "lifelong rage against her father," who, Lee writes, was also "the love of her life." (Lee, 148, 149)

> She was in love with him; she was furious with him; she was like him; she never stopped arguing with him; and when she finally read Freud in 1939, she recognized exactly what he meant by "ambivalence." (Lee, 68)

Lee cites Woolf's own diary entry of November 28, 1928, wherein Woolf wrote that if her father had continued to live, "his life would have entirely ended mine.... No writing, no books;—inconceivable." (Lee, 68) The reason was simply that in his domestic relations, which, in his family, essentially meant in his relations with women, Stephen was emotionally voracious and tyrannical, egotistically demanding and insatiable. When his wife died he transferred his neediness and expectations of servitude onto his stepdaughter, Julia's daughter from her first marriage Stella Duckworth; and when Stella died two years later, he transferred the burden of serving him to his daughter Vanessa. Like Charles Ramsay in *To the Lighthouse*, he was particularly distressed by a sense of himself as a failure despite the quantity and influence of his work during his lifetime, fearing his work would not last and that he would not be preserved in the ranks of genius. From the vantage point of over a hundred years since his death, he seems to have been right in his estimate. We know him not because of his own work but because he was Virginia Woolf's father.

In a sketch of him she made towards the end of her life, Woolf showed her own sense of the value of his work and the strength of his capabilities and offered an implicit contrast of his sensibility and her own:

> When I read his books I get a critical grasp of him; I always read *Hours in a Library* by way of filling out my ideas, say of

Coleridge, if I'm reading Coleridge; and always find something to fill out; to correct; to stiffen my fluid vision. I find not a subtle mind; not an imaginative mind; not a suggestive mind. But a strong mind; a healthy out of door, moor striding mind; an impatient, limited mind; a conventional mind entirely accepting his own standard of what is honest, what is moral.... I get a sense of Leslie Stephen, the muscular agnostic; cheery, hearty; always cracking up sense and manliness; and crying down sentimentality and vagueness.... I admire (laughingly) that Leslie Stephen; and sometimes lately have envied him. Yet he is not a writer for whom I have a natural taste. Yet just as a dog takes a bite of grass, I take a bite of him medicinally, and there often steals in, not a filial, but a reader's affection for him; for his courage, his simplicity, for his strength and nonchalance, and neglect of appearances. (Lee, 71)

Despite the measured cadence of her prose, Woolf leaves the impression that she has less of a reader's distance from Leslie Stephen and more the ambivalent mix of aggression and dependency which often marks the nature of children's affection for their parents. Sir Francis Bacon, it will be recalled, recommended tasting some books and chewing others, but never taking a bite out of the author.

In one form or another, Leslie Stephen reappears in Woolf's novels. Mr. Hilberry in *Night and Day* edits a review and cultivates young writers. He is essentially a good-hearted man absorbed in his own work. He is on the periphery of the novel, withdrawn from involvement with the complexities of the plot, which proceeds for the most part without him until he is forced to exert his authority. And then he is rather at a loss, reverts to conventional values and tyrannical methods, and muddles things with his blind authoritarianism until his wife, returning early from a pilgrimage to Shakespeare's tomb, straightens things out.

Colonel Pargiter in *The Years* is a grumpy, moody *paterfamilias* who dominates his large family, sometimes fascinating them with his charm, sometimes stifling them with his gloom:

He was always at his best in the evening; he enjoyed his dinner; and for some reason his gloom had vanished. He was in his jovial mood. His children's spirits rose as they noted it.

"That's a pretty frock you're wearing," he said to Delia as he sat down.

"This old one?" she said, patting the blue muslin.

There was an opulence, an ease and a charm about him when he was in a good temper that she liked particularly. People always said she was like him; sometimes she was glad of it—tonight for instance. He looked so pink and clean and genial in his dinner-jacket. They became children again when he was in this mood, and were spurred on to make family jokes at which they all laughed for no particular reason.

Then Woolf shifts the point of view away from omniscient narrative:

Delia liked listening to her father's stories about India. They were crisp, and at the same time romantic....

He used always to be like this when we were small, she thought. He used to jump over the bonfire on her birthday, she remembered. She watched him flicking cutlets dexterously on to plates with his left hand. [He had lost two fingers on his right hand during military service.] She admired his decision, his common sense. (Woolf, *The Years*, 35–36)

His temperament is formative and influences the lives and dispositions of his children even after his death.

It is, however, Charles Ramsey in *To the Lighthouse* who is the most developed and complex of the figures drawn from Leslie Stephen. Charles Ramsay is a brilliant philosopher and a successful writer. He has many admirers and has made a solid contribution to philosophy. But he has a moody, nagging sense of self-doubt about the magnitude of his importance, which is also a form of pride or vanity, and he needs continuous reassurance, which must essentially take the form of nearly worshipful, submissive admiration, whether for his intellectual contribution or for the beauty of his boots. (Woolf, *Lighthouse*, 174) Although there are many characters in *To the Lighthouse*—Mrs. Ramsay, his wife, chief among them, and the painter, Lily Brascoe, too—who are limned with care, precision and suggestiveness—more so, perhaps, than he is—nevertheless, they are drawn in relation to him, as they submit to him, or defy him, or do both simultaneously.

The essential matter, the organizing principle, of *To the Lighthouse* is his effect on all the other characters, their sense of themselves and the feelings they have, how he determines their psychic existence. Woolf's working title for the book, indeed, was "The Old Man." His son, James, is defined in the first pages of the book by his father's spiteful (but accurate—so much worse does that make his power) contradiction of his hope for good weather on the following day so that they might go to the lighthouse across from their summer house. The hatred James feels for his father because of the pressure of his father's personality upon his own remains with him still ten years later when they finally do sail to the lighthouse. James's sister, Cam, is defined in the last section of the novel, when she is sailing to the lighthouse with her father and her brother, by ambivalence for her father, which surely has as its source Virginia Woolf's ambivalent relation to Leslie Stephen:

> [N]o one attracted her more; his hands were beautiful to her and his feet, and his voice, and his words, and his haste, and his temper, and his oddity, and his passion ... and his remoteness.... But what remained intolerable, she thought ... was that crass blindness and tyranny of his which had poisoned her childhood and raised bitter storms, so that even now she awoke in the night trembling with rage and remembered some command of his; some insolence: "Do this", "Do that"; his dominance: his "Submit to me". (Woolf, *Lighthouse*, 193)

It is the particular heroism of Mrs. Ramsay that she can both love her husband but retain a delicate integrity which keeps her from cheapening that love by saying "I love you" to him when he needs it for vain satisfaction, so that it remains love and does not become submission. (Woolf, *Lighthouse*, 142) Woolf's manner of presenting Mr. Ramsay, just because of his centrality to the consciousness and definition of the other characters in the novel and because they reciprocally are necessary to him for his sense of himself, relies on a narrative developed through the complex interaction of multiple perspectives and of multiple subjective perceptions. He exists for the reader as he thinks about himself and reacts to himself and as other characters think about and react to him. Similarly, Mrs. Ramsay exists for the reader as she is perceived by and thought about by others as well as by her own perceptions of others and herself.

Using a lighter tone and a fantastic narrative, but actually with no less serious intent, Woolf establishes Alexander Pope, as he appears in *Orlando*, her great comic anatomy of gender, literature, fashion, and history, as a father figure regarding whom Orlando experiences a similar ambivalence, causing her feelings to ricochet between veneration and contempt as the carriage in which the two of them are riding one evening passes through alternating stretches of light and darkness. (Woolf, *Orlando*, 204–206)

Julia Stephen, Woolf's mother, was obviously a strong woman with a forceful character, even if it had to be expressed within the confines of a feminine sensibility as defined by Victorian convention. She bore seven children, cared selflessly for the sick, wrote a great deal, and, like Mrs. Ramsay, devoted herself to the satisfaction of a voraciously needy and often gloomy husband. She, too, like Leslie Stephen, is a recurring character in Woolf's fiction, and her circumstances a recurring theme. She is reflected not only in Mrs. Ramsay, but in the shadowy figure of the dying Mrs. Pargiter in *The Years* and in Clarissa Dalloway in *Mrs. Dalloway*, too. Like Mrs. Ramsay, she died leaving young children behind her. The effect of her death on Virginia was terrible, and, according to Woolf, it "brought on ... my first 'breakdown.'" (Lee, 178)

Woolf's two half-brothers, Gerald and George Duckworth, both violated her sexually. Gerald was the first. Virginia was a child, not yet an adolescent. She described the attack in 1939:

> There was a slab outside the dining room door for standing dishes upon. Once when I was very small Gerald Duckworth lifted me onto this, and as I sat there he began to explore my body. I can remember the feel of his hand going under my clothes; going firmly and steadily lower and lower. I remember how I hoped that he would stop; how I stiffened and wriggled as his hand approached my private parts. But it did not stop. His hand explored my private parts too. I

remember resenting, disliking it—what is the word for so
dumb and mixed a feeling? It must have been strong, since I
still recall it. (Lee, 125)

Woolf not only suffered and resented the assault but felt ashamed and
guilty herself with regard to it. That this is a common phenomenon does
not make it any less powerful in each individual instance. For Woolf, it
is yet another aspect of her life that caused division in her. She identified
herself as both the object of violence and the agent of shame and guilt
for the violation. Gerald, moreover, played more than one role in her
life: he published her first two novels at the Duckworth Press.

In her adolescence and young womanhood, Virginia's other half-
brother, George, exercised great authority over her, took her out into
the society of his friends—not literary, but political people—and
intensely sexualized their relationship. Lee writes,

The nights of dressing up and going out with George ended
... with George helping her undress, or coming into the
bedroom after she was undressed, lying on her bed and
fondling her. (Lee, 153–154)

The contradictions in her circumstances and the inevitable
confusion of her reactions found expression in the division of her
character as manifest in her mental breakdowns, in her mature fiction,
and in her politics. Sometimes, she could put her experience of
fragmentation to profound use, as in her art and thought; sometimes it
overcame her. She encompassed both possibilities. Like her work, her
mental turmoil is characterized by fragmentation and vacillation
between polar extremes. Leonard Woolf, writing in the 1960s,
characterized Woolf's illness this way:

In the manic stage she was extremely excited; the mind raced;
she talked volubly and, at the height of the attack,
incoherently, she had delusions and heard voices.... [S]he was
violent with her nurses.... During the depressive stage all her
thoughts and emotions were the exact opposite of what they
had been in the manic stage. She was in the depths of
melancholia and despair; she scarcely spoke; refused to eat;

refused to believe that she was really ill and insisted that her condition was due to her own guilt. (Lee, 178–179)

In her fiction Woolf succeeded in doing what eluded her in her madness. Her particular art is the successful formal integration of fragments (of consciousness, of perception, of voices, of narratives, of multiple and varying perspectives) by the construction of a complex narrative consciousness with the power to encompass opposing forces.

MRS. DALLOWAY

In her novels, Virginia Woolf uses conflicting, even irreconcilable, elements in the construction of characters and dramatic situations. She uses the multiple perspectives of the characters' perceptions to create dramatic tension among characters and a sense of the elusiveness of human character. She shapes narrative by shifting from one point of view to another rather than by expressing only a single dominant and dominating narrator's voice.

There is a scene in Virginia Woolf's fourth novel, *Mrs. Dalloway* (1925), which very clearly shows the complexity of Woolf's artistic vision. Mrs. Dalloway is awakened from an afternoon nap on the couch in the drawing room by the entrance of her seventeen-year-old daughter, Elizabeth. Elizabeth has just finished her history lesson, and her tutor, Miss Kilman, is waiting for her outside on the landing. They are about to go shopping. Miss Kilman has used her place as Elizabeth's teacher to influence her emotionally and intellectually, playing on the unshaped idealism of youth, firing her with a self-abnegating passion for Christianity. The effect has been to alienate Elizabeth from her parents, whose wealth and class comfort Miss Kilman resents. Miss Kilman's religious enthusiasm serves as the vehicle for both expressing and containing her overwhelming sense of embittered self-pity and resentment, her "grudge against the world." (Woolf, *Mrs. Dalloway*, 195) Miss Kilman felt

[s]he had been cheated. Yes, the word was no exaggeration, for surely a girl has a right to some kind of happiness? And she had never been happy, what with being so clumsy and so

poor. And then, just as she might have had a chance at Miss
Dolby's school, the war came; and she never had been able to
tell lies. Miss Dolby thought she would be happier with
people who shared her views about the Germans. She had
had to go. It was true that the family was of German origin;
spelt the name Kiehlman in the eighteenth century; but her
brother had been killed. They turned her out because she
would not pretend that the Germans were all villains—when
she had German friends, when the only happy days of her life
had been spent in Germany! And after all, she could read
history. She had had to take whatever she could get. Mr.
Dalloway had come across her working for the Friends. He
had allowed her (and that was really generous of him) to
teach his daughter history. Also she did a little Extension
lecturing and so on. Then Our Lord had come to her (and
here she always bowed her head). She had seen the light two
years and three months ago. Now she did not envy women
like Clarissa Dalloway; she pitied them.

   She pitied and despised them from the bottom of her
heart, as she stood on the soft carpet, looking at the old
engraving of a little girl with a muff. With all this luxury
going on, what hope was there for a better state of things?
Instead of lying on a sofa—"My mother is resting," Elizabeth
had said—she should have been in a factory; behind a
counter; Mrs. Dalloway and all the other fine ladies! (Woolf,
Mrs. Dalloway, 187–188)

These paragraphs do not record the objective voice of a narrator
but a narrative intervention, bringing to the surface the thoughts,
feelings, and attitudes of Miss Kilman. It is not just information about
her that is introduced, but the tortured tone of her being is represented.
Moreover, the narrative method establishes more than what she is
"thinking." It imitates and represents what she is projecting as she
stands before Clarissa Dalloway—what Mrs. Dalloway sees—even if she
is silent.

   Mrs. Dalloway is repelled by Miss Kilman, not just because of Miss
Kilman's scorn for her, or for her baleful influence on Elizabeth, but
because her physical presence, her attitude, and the very way she dresses

all declare her bitterness, resentment, doctrinaire righteousness, and human isolation. Nevertheless Clarissa Dalloway goes out onto the landing with Elizabeth to greet Miss Kilman. She is able to just because of the aspects of her personality which are the opposite of Miss Kilman's. She is gracious and self-effacing, and she has a sense that the personal supersedes the doctrinal. Even as she is subject to Miss Kilman's glowering scorn, Mrs. Dalloway maintains a generosity of spirit although she sees clearly the wretched core of Miss Kilman's nature. Mrs. Dalloway sees Miss Kilman as "[t]his woman" who "had taken her daughter from her!" She finds her "[h]eavey, ugly, commonplace, without kindness or grace." Nevertheless,

> as Miss Kilman stood there (and stand she did, with the power and taciturnity of some prehistoric monster armoured for primeval warfare), how, second by second, the idea of her diminished, how hatred (which was for ideas, not people) crumbled, how she lost her malignity, her size, became second by second merely Miss Kilman, in a mackintosh, whom Heaven knows Clarissa would have liked to help.
>
> At this dwindling of the monster, Clarissa laughed. Saying good-bye, she laughed. (Woolf, *Mrs. Dalloway*, 190)

For Mrs. Dalloway, hatred can exist only in regard to ideas, not people. Miss Kilman uses ideas to reinforce and justify her animosity.

Clarissa, clearly, is not laughing at Miss Kilman. Her laugh signifies the relief and pleasure she feels at being able to overcome her hatred for Miss Kilman, at not being caught by the possibility of denying Miss Kilman's humanity because of hatred that tempts her to see her as a monster. But Miss Kilman understands the laugh differently. Self-pitying, she interprets the laugh as an insult:

> Clarissa Dalloway had insulted her. That she expected. But she [Miss Kilman] had not triumphed; she [Miss Kilman] had not mastered the flesh. Ugly, clumsy, Clarissa Dalloway had laughed at her for being that [ugly and clumsy]; and had revived the fleshly desires, for she minded looking as she did beside Clarissa. Nor could she [Miss Kilman] talk as she [Clarissa] did. But why wish to resemble her? Why?

She despised Mrs. Dalloway from the bottom of her heart. She was not serious. She was not good. Her life was a tissue of vanity and deceit. Yet Doris Kilman had been overcome. She had, as a matter of fact, very nearly burst into tears when Clarissa Dalloway laughed at her.... Clarissa Dalloway had laughed—but she would concentrate her mind upon something else until she had reached the pillar-box. At any rate she had got Elizabeth. (Woolf, *Mrs. Dalloway*, 194–195)

So Mrs. Dalloway was right in her assessment of Miss Kilman. Miss Kilman's attachment to Elizabeth is an aggressive one, reflecting resentment and revenge, not affection or care. As it turns out, Miss Kilman has not "got Elizabeth," for the girl is young and the freshness of her spirit balks at the stale confinement of Miss Kilman's asceticism, self-centered bitterness, and self-pity, but that is less thematically relevant than Clarissa Dalloway's thoughts after the two set off on their shopping trip and she is once again alone:

Love and religion! thought Clarissa, going back into the drawing-room, tingling all over. How detestable, how detestable they are! For now that the body of Miss Kilman was not before her, it overwhelmed her—the idea. The cruelest things in the world, she thought, seeing them clumsy, hot, domineering, hypocritical, eavesdropping, jealous, infinitely cruel and unscrupulous, dressed in a mackintosh coat, on the landing; love and religion. Had she ever tried to convert any one herself? Did she not wish everybody merely to be themselves? (Woolf, *Mrs. Dalloway*, 191)

Compare this passage with one which occurs earlier in *Mrs. Dalloway* about

a Goddess even now engaged—in the heat and sands of India, the mud and swamp of Africa, the purlieus of London, wherever in short the climate or the devil tempts men to fall from the true belief which is her own—is even now engaged in dashing down shrines, smashing idols, and setting up in their place her own stern countenance. Conversion is her name and she feasts on the wills of the weakly, loving to impress, to impose, adoring her own features stamped on the face of the populace. At Hyde Park Corner on a tub she stands preaching; shrouds herself in white and walks penitentially disguised as brotherly love through factories and parliaments; offers help, but desires power; smites out of her way roughly the dissentient, or dissatisfied; bestows her blessing on those who, looking upward, catch submissively from her eyes the light of their own. (Woolf, *Mrs. Dalloway*, 151)

This passage follows Septimus Smith's encounter with William Bradshaw. Septimus is a young man returned from the First World War who is haunted by the trauma of having seen a friend blown up in the war. Bradshaw is the specialist his wife brings him to consult about his despondency and the hallucinations which accompany it. Blind to the delicacy of the human organism, obtuse in his belief in his own vision of life, Bradshaw sees Septimus as having lost his sense of "proportion" and "order[s[rest in bed; rest in solitude; silence and rest; rest without friends, without books, without messages; six months' rest; until a man who went in weighing seven stone six comes out weighing twelve." (Woolf, *Mrs. Dalloway*, 150) This is the same treatment that Woolf herself was made to undergo. Its chief strategy is to deny the validity of the tormented experience and to impose the will of the physician upon the psyche of the sufferer.

The passion for converting others, for imposing oneself and one's will on another, and the certainty that one is right in doing so and has the right to do so, is opposed by Clarissa Dalloway's epiphany as she stands by her window after Miss Kilman and her daughter are gone. She sees the woman across the way alone in her room and grasps that there is one inviolable, impenetrable "supreme mystery," that there is a "privacy of the soul," that "here is one room; there another"(Woolf, *Mrs. Dalloway*, 192, 193), and that we are bound to one another's separateness in and in spite of our differences and violate one another when we try to force one will, one pattern of thought, one rule of behavior universally.

The Force of Power vs. the Power of Withdrawing

If there are villains in *Mrs. Dalloway*, they are Sir William Bradshaw and Miss Kilman—her name certainly suggests misanthropy. Bradshaw is a personality drawn from the doctors who treated Woolf during her periods of mental breakdown, for whom she had unreserved contempt and loathing. Clarissa Dalloway intuitively dislikes him. Septimus Smith, rather than surrender himself to Bradshaw and confinement, "had thrown himself from a window." (Woolf, *Mrs. Dalloway*, 280) It is an act with which Woolf's own ultimate suicide shows she has great sympathy. Within the context of the novel, when Clarissa Dalloway, who did not know Septimus Smith, hears the story of Septimus's suicide at her party that evening from Sir William, one of her guests, with great accuracy she imagines how Bradshaw must have affected Septimus Smith:

> Suppose he had had that passion, and had gone to Sir William Bradshaw, a great doctor yet to her obscurely evil, without sex or lust, extremely polite to women, but capable of some indescribable outrage—forcing your soul, that was it—if this young man had gone to him, and Sir William had impressed him, like that, with his power, might he not then have said (indeed she felt it now), Life is made intolerable; they make life intolerable, men like that? (Woolf, *Mrs. Dalloway*, 281)

It is more difficult to characterize Miss Kilman as a villain, whether drawing on internal or external information. Inside the novel, there are mitigating circumstances. A reader can understand why she is the way she is—in Clarissa's mind, "hypocritical, corrupt; with all that power; the woman who had crept in to steal and defile." (Woolf, *Mrs. Dalloway*, 266) Miss Kilman has been cursed by nature by:

> the infliction of [an] unlovable body which people could not bear to see. Do her hair as she might, her forehead remained like an egg, bald white. No clothes suited her.... And for a woman, of course, that meant never meeting the opposite sex. Never would she come first with any one. (Woolf, *Mrs. Dalloway*, 195)

When she feels cheated, moreover, for having been fired because she would not get caught up in blind anti-German sentiment during the First World War, she is accurate in her feelings. Moreover, in many ways, Miss Kilman stands for things that Virginia Woolf herself stood for politically and culturally, and Clarissa Dalloway follows in a tradition from which Woolf sought liberation. Like Miss Kilman, Woolf was a pacifist, and remained one even in time of war. In *Three Guineas* (1938), arguing the case for the end of sexual discrimination against women and against war, Woolf insists on the need for women to have the same work opportunities as men, and in the third section of the book Woolf argues against nationalism and for erasing ideas of difference between people based on whether they are "English" or "German." She encourages women rather to think of themselves as "Outsiders." (Woolf, *Three Guineas*, 156, 162, 164–165)

Clarissa Dalloway, in many ways like Mrs. Ramsay and Woolf's own mother—living for others and strong in their integrity—is of the type of woman Woolf called "the angel in the house," after a figure in the novel of that name by Coventry Patmore. It is a figure Woolf wants to overthrow, and Woolf herself, writing in her own voice often shows the aggressive passion of Miss Kilman (and the spirit of Mr. Rochester's mad wife in the attic in *Jane Eyre*) rather than the wise disposition for understanding and reconciliation embodied in Mrs. Dalloway or Mrs. Ramsay:

> Take this guinea and with it burn the college to the ground.
> Set fire to the old hypocrisies. Let the light of the burning
> buildings scare the nightingales and incarnadine the willows.
> And let the daughters of educated men dance round the fire
> and heap armfuls of dead leaves upon the flames. And let
> their mothers lean from the upper windows and cry, "Let it
> blaze! Let it blaze! For we have done with this education"!
> (Woolf, *Three Guineas*, 53)

Clearly, however, Woolf also believes that Mrs. Dalloway's and Mrs. Ramsay's qualities of spiritual generosity and compassion, their ability to identify with others and, without surrendering their own dignity, care for others, is of deep value. It also has a price. Mrs. Ramsay dies; Mrs. Dalloway has the quietness of one who has suffered a subduing illness. And although Miss Kilman represents much that Woolf wishes to see predominate—educated, self-supporting women, challenging the narrowness of nationalism and the validity of war—she is presented as a figure doomed by her faults, by her resentment. Her decency is subverted by her own status as an outsider, not burnished by it. In her the need to change social conditions becomes the malicious desire to make converts, to gain that power over others that one obtains when others renounce their desires in favor of one's own. The complexity of vision that enables Woolf to create such complex characters is at the foundation of her art and prevents her ideas from overpowering either her art or her thought, or the political from subverting the aesthetic, and turning literature into propaganda.

And yet, as noted above, the reader can understand Miss Kilman, and, like Mrs. Dalloway, have a sense of compassion for her, and have a sense of humanity aggrieved in her, because she is a creation of art, not of propaganda, presented from within, as consciousness and perception; for Woolf, in her novels, is concerned to reveal the complexity of humanity. *Three Guineas* is a tract, not a novel, which is designed, however artfully, entirely to further a purpose: to uncover the causes of war in the patriarchal suppression of women. Its avowed purpose is "to assert 'the rights of all—all men and women—to the respect in their persons of the great principles of Justice, Equality, and Liberty.'" (Woolf, *Three Guineas*, 219) In a note at the end of that tract, referring to *Antigone*, the final play of Sophocles's Oedipus cycle, Woolf writes:

> [W]hen the curtain falls we sympathize ... even with [the tyrant] Creon himself. This result, to the propagandist undesirable, would seem to be due to the fact that Sophocles ... uses freely all the faculties that can be possessed by a writer; and suggests therefore, that if we use art to propagate political opinions, we must force the artist to clip and cabin his gift to do us a cheap and passing service. Literature will suffer the same mutation that the mule has suffered; and there will be no more horses. (Woolf, *Three Guineas*, 259)

Nevertheless, the reader may object, after finishing *Mrs. Dalloway*, that in imagining the character of Sir William Bradford Woolf was untrue to her artistic integrity. He is entirely unsympathetic. His humanity is subsumed by his indomitable authority, which, Woolf notes, is backed up by the police (Woolf, *Mrs. Dalloway*, 154), and which can only be evaded if one is unable to abandon oneself to him and submit by committing suicide, as Septimus Smith does.

Bradshaw, indeed, is not drawn as a complex figure whose humanity is explored as it might be, even if only in quest of uncovering what leads to the formation of a tyrannical personality and makes the exercise of tyrannical authority satisfying. Bradshaw exists in *Mrs. Dalloway* as a defining social force, a force that all Woolf's work seems written to examine, deconstruct, and defuse, the force of domination that tries to set limits on experience or to assert power against it.

THE TYRANNY OF FACT VS. THE HUMANITY OF PERCEPTION

A recurrent theme in Woolf's work is the tension between resistance and capitulation to a powerful force of will which is devoted to accomplishing the submission of the other and to asserting its own dominance. It is, as we have seen, what characterizes such differing figures as Colonel Pargiter, William Bradshaw, and Charles Ramsay. Its personal origin for Woolf was in the figure of her father, Leslie Stephen. Abstracted and generalized from her experience of life with him, it is the force of patriarchal authority, which Woolf understood to be at the root of social injustice and brutality as well as of individual or domestic unhappiness. Woolf was not doctrinaire about this. She did not see patriarchal authority as the sole possible evil or believe that evil was gender-determined, but rather that patriarchy was the established, existing, and operative source of injustice, suffering, and oppression. Her approach as a writer to undermine patriarchal domination, and indeed to subvert all forms of authoritarianism, was twofold, involving the formalism of her aesthetics as well as the content of her thought.

The idea embodied in the form of Virginia Woolf's novels is that truth is not a monolithic moral absolute which can emanate from one particular and fixed source; nor are we single-minded in our perception or without ambivalence in our experience. Even our existence of time is not bound only to the objective present. The present occasion often releases impressions of the past and fantasies about the future. Truth inheres, then, in the fluidity of a multi-perspectived perception with an ever-shifting spacial and temporal center; thus it can have no dominant point of authority or definition. This apparently anti-moral attack on fixed truth in itself, paradoxically, asserts a moral proposition. It is perhaps most succinctly demonstrated in a scene between Charles and Mrs. Ramsay regarding their son James's childish hope that he will be able go to the lighthouse the following day and his father's callous disregard for the boy's sensitivity by his unnecessary insistence that the weather will be bad and the trip impossible. Mr. Ramsay has fact on his side. But the human truth is lodged not in fact but in the awareness of the interrelation of the fact and the person at whom it is directed. This sensitivity is expressed by Mrs. Ramsay, but only to herself, in her thoughts, rebelling against her husband's tyrannical truthfulness:

> There wasn't the slightest possible chance that they could go to the Lighthouse tomorrow, Mr Ramsay snapped out irascibly.
> How did he know? she asked. The wind often changed.
> The extraordinary irrationality of her remark, the folly of women's minds enraged him.... "Damn you," he said. But what had she said? Simply that it might be fine tomorrow. So it might.
> Not with the barometer falling and the wind due west.
> To pursue truth with such astonishing lack of consideration for other people's feelings, to rend the thin veils of civilization so wantonly, so brutally, was to her [Mrs. Ramsay] so horrible an outrage of human decency that, without replying, dazed and blinded, she bent her head as if to let the pelt of jagged hail, the drench of dirty water, bespatter her unrebuked. There was nothing to be said. (Woolf, *Lighthouse*, 37–38)

Mrs. Ramsay's sensitivity is formally reiterated in *To the Lighthouse* by its narrative scheme, which is not straightforward or objective or authoritative, but follows the way reality is subjectively perceived from the points of view of a number of characters. Moreover, reality is not in *To the Lighthouse* a matter of fact, but of impression.

Erich Auerbach's analysis of a scene in *To the Lighthouse* which ends
with a narrative comment about Mrs. Ramsay—"Never did anyone
look so sad"—problematizes Woolf's narrative voice:

> Who is speaking in this paragraph? Who is looking at Mrs.
> Ramsay here, who concludes that never did anybody look so
> sad? Who is expressing these doubtful, obscure
> suppositions? ... There is no one near the window in the
> room but Mrs. Ramsay and James. It cannot be either of
> them, nor the "people" who begin to speak in the next
> paragraph. Perhaps it is the author. However, if that be so,
> the author certainly does not speak like one who has a
> knowledge of his characters—in this case, of Mrs. Ramsay—
> and who, out of his knowledge, can describe their personality
> and momentary state of mind objectively and with certainty.
> Virginia Woolf wrote this paragraph. She did not identify it
> through grammatical and typographical devices as the
> speech or thought of a third person. One is obliged to
> assume that it contains direct statements of her own. But she
> does not seem to bear in mind that she is the author and
> hence ought to know how matters stand with her characters.
> The person speaking here, whoever it is, acts the part of one
> who has only an impression of Mrs. Ramsay. (Auerbach, 469)

Through the character of Lily Briscoe and using the art of
painting Woolf actually exposes her formal strategy in writing. Woolf's
work from the start had been greatly influenced by Post-Impressionism.
"The Post-Impressionist movement had cast—not its shadow—but its
bunch of variegated light upon us," she wrote. (Bernard, 16) The
Bloomsbury circle was, in fact, as much a group of painters and art
critics as it was of literary people. Clive Bell, Roger Fry, Duncan Grant,
and Woolf's sister, Vanessa Bell, were all painters. In 1910, it was Fry
who organized an exhibition of Post-Impressionist painters—Cezanne,
Van Gogh, Matisse, Gauguin, Braque, and Picasso—in London, and in
1912 he organized a second such exhibit, this time including the work of
Vanessa and Clive Bell and Duncan Grant alongside theirs. One of the
commanding tenets of Post-Impressionist Modernism, formulated by
Roger Fry, guides Woolf's work: "[T]he assumption that fidelity to

appearance [is] the measure of art [has] no logical foundation[;] ... the question of art begins where the question of fact ends." (Bernard, 20) Thus truth, as Woolf argued later in her criticism of the Edwardian novelists Wells, Bennett, and Galsworthy, is something spiritual, and not necessarily embodied, as Mrs. Ramsay knows, in fact or appearance. "The meaning of a book," Woolf writes in a discussion of Charlotte Brontë's genius, "lies so often apart from what happens and what is said ... and itself [may be] rather a mood than a particular observation." (Woolf, "Jane Eyre", 224–225)

Thus, in the first section of *To the Lighthouse*, Lily Briscoe, a painter and summer guest, has set up her easel on the lawn and is working on a landscape which includes Mrs. Ramsay and James. She is interrupted by William Bankes, another houseguest, who looks at her unfinished picture:

> It was Mrs Ramsay reading to James, she said. She knew his objection—that no one could tell it for a human shape. But she had made no attempt at likeness, she said. For what reason had she introduced them then? ... Why indeed?— except that if there, in that corner, it was bright, here, in this, she felt the need of darkness.... Mother and child then— objects of universal veneration, and in this case the mother was famous for her beauty—might be reduced, he pondered, to a purple shadow without irreverence.
>
> But the picture was not of them, she said. Or, not in his sense. There were other senses too in which one might reverence them. By a shadow here and a light there, for instance.... A mother and child might be reduced to a shadow without irreverence. A light here required a shadow there .... The question being one of the relations of masses, of lights and shadows.... It was a question, she remembered, how to connect this mass on the right hand with that on the left. She might do it by bringing the line of the branch across so; or break the vacancy in the foreground by an object (James perhaps) so. (Woolf, *Lighthouse*, 61–62)

CODA

The effect of Woolf's recomposition of reality, sacrificing authorial command to phenomenological impressionism, can often make her work difficult, especially at the first reading, for there is no guide to orient the reader. A second, even a third, reading is necessary in order for the pieces to become organized into some meaningful constellation and for the whole to gain resonance and meaning—for the melodies, harmonies, and tonal colorings to emerge—for the figures to shape themselves in our minds. Thus, after several readings of *Jacob's Room*, the reader becomes aware that the substance of the book primarily exists in the scenes the reader does not see, in the conversations that are about to happen and suggest themselves, but are not transcribed, in letters that are left unread. It is a book about a young man killed in the First World War, about a life suggested, but unrealized. *The Years*, similarly, is a book from which content has been drained and in which narrative development is continually being interrupted, as are the lives of the women who populate the novel. They are women who live burdened by the fact that patriarchy has robbed their lives of substance, even as they continue to live and experience from year to year as sentient, intelligent beings with memory, desire, hope, frustration, and loss. *The Waves* is stripped entirely of all authorial scaffolding, and the reader must construct the novel from the six monologues issuing from the six characters, which chart their consciousness of their lives.

What Woolf as a writer, then, requires of her reader is the capacity to integrate, to constellate disparities into unities. At the end of *A Room of One's Own* her hope is that overcoming patriarchal consciousness, and therefore the oppression she argues it engenders, will allow for the assimilation of the male and the female aspects of consciousness. Indeed, at the heart of the conceit that governs *Orlando* is the supposition that gender identity is as much a fact of consciousness as it is of physiology, if not more so. In the great fantasia that concludes *Orlando* she announces that there are "sixty or seventy different times that beat simultaneously in every normal human system" and that "nothing is any longer one thing." (Woolf, *Orlando*, 304). "Everything," she proclaims, is "partly something else, and each gain[s] an odd moving power from this union of itself and something not itself." (Woolf, *Orlando*, 323)

NOTES

1. Often a daunting concept, phenomenology, a philosophical system devised by Edmund Husserl at the beginning of the twentieth century, is the study of the observation of things as they are—without ideas about them—which means as they are perceived. Consequently, the nature of the thing perceived and the perceiving subject are interdependent. The perceived takes its identity and definition from the perceiver. Subjective perception, moreover, is considered to be all there is. The concept of phenomenology is in contrast to the idea that things have an objective existence independent of any perception of them.

Here is an example, from Woolf's last novel, *Between the Acts*, of a phenomenological description: "The flower blazed between the angles of the roots. Membrane after membrane was torn. It blazed a soft yellow, a lambent light under a film of velvet; it filled the caverns behind the eyes with light. All that inner darkness became a hall, leaf smelling, earth smelling, of yellow light, and the tree was beyond the flower; the grass, the flower and the tree were entire. Down on his knees grubbing he held the flower complete." (Harcourt, Brace, and Company, 1941, p. 11)

2. Queen Victoria reigned from 1837 through 1901. Her successor, King Edward VII, died in 1910.

WORKS CITED

Auerbach, Erich. *Mimesis: The Representation of Reality in Western Literature.* Garden City, N.Y.: Doubleday Anchor Books, 2003.

Bernard, C., and C. Reynier. *V. Woolf: The Waves.* Paris: Didier Erudition— CNED, 1995.

Lee, Hermione. *Virginia Woolf.* London: Chato & Windus, 1996.

Woolf, Virginia. "*Jane Eyre* and *Wuthering Heights.*" *The Common Reader.* New York: Harcourt, Brace, and Company, 1925.

———. "Modern Fiction." *The Common Reader,* New York: Harcourt, Brace, and Company, 1925.

———. *Orlando.* New York: Harcourt, Brace, and Company, 1993.

———. *The Years.* New York: Harcourt, Brace, and Company, 1969.

———. *To the Lighthous.* Middlesex, England: Penguin Books, 1989.

———. *Mrs. Dalloway.* New York: Harcourt, Brace, and Company, 1990.

———. *Three Guineas.* New York: Harcourt, Brace, and Company, 1963.

GEORGE ELLA LYON

Virginia Woolf and
the Problem of the Body

> I know of no woman ... for whom her body is not a fundamental problem....
> —Adrienne Rich, *Of Woman Born*[1]

> Who shall measure the heat and violence of the poet's heart when caught and tangled in a woman's body?
> —*A Room of One's Own*, p. 83

Being female is a problem by definition because the definitions are not the female's own. She is, as Virginia Woolf says, "perhaps, the most discussed animal in the universe" (*ROO*, p. 44). Set apart, idealized, feared, she is pure slut, brainless witch, mother death. Caught in this thicket of definitions, contradictory and dehumanizing, a girl may retreat from life altogether and may retreat from her body itself. This second retreat enables her, in male terms, to rise above herself, to concentrate. It appears to free her from what Adrienne Rich calls the "clouded meaning" of her body, "its fertility, its desire, its so-called frigidity, its bloody speech, its silences, its changes and mutilations, its rapes and ripenings."[2]

 In this world which defines woman as *object*, as less than and at the disposal of man, Virginia Woolf the artist must define herself as *subject* in

From *Virginia Woolf: Centennial Essays*, ed. Elaine K. Ginsberg and Laura Moss Gottlieb. © 1983 by The Whitston Publishing Company. Reprinted by permission.

95

order to write.[3] Her fictional vision has been described by James
Naremore as one of the "world without a self,"[4] and it is true that often
her characters have acute difficulty in possessing themselves. Possessed
by the world around them (Rachel Vinrace, Septimus Warren Smith,
Rhoda in *The Waves*), so tenuously moored in themselves, they cannot
risk entering and being entered by the realities of other people (Clarissa
Dalloway, Rachel, St. John Hirst, William Dodge). If we see Woolf as a
woman defined as *object* struggling to become and to remain *subject* (as
she herself describes in "Professions for Women," *DM*, p. 235–242), the
portent of her characters' struggles becomes clearer.

Aware of her beauty from an early age, Virginia Woolf recalls in "A
Sketch of the Past" the ambiguous feelings her pleasure in it caused her.
"The looking-glass shame," as she calls it, is connected with Gerald
Duckworth's unwanted exploration of her body. But she also says that, in
relation to herself, her "natural love for beauty" may have been "checked
by some ancestral dread." Her father was, after all, "spartan, ascetic,
puritanical," and he was the head of the family, the writer, the one with
the power to "give her away" in marriage (*MB*, p. 68).

Because of history, circumstance, and temperament, Julia Stephen
was "a general presence" rather than "a particular person" to her
daughter. "Can I remember ever being alone with her for more than a
few minutes?" Woolf asks in "A Sketch of the Past." And she answers,
"When I think of her spontaneously she is always in a room full of
people ..." (*MB*, p. 83). So the girl's world turned around an unreachable
center. At her mother's death when she was thirteen, even that distant
center disappeared. Woolf was left in a world spinning out of place. It is
not surprising, then, that motherlessness permeates her characters
(Rachel, Clarissa, James and Cam, Lily, the family in *The Years*), and it is
important in considering her sense of her own embodiment that she was
unmothered not only once, and at a crucial age, but twice, and that these
unmotherings are woven with the shock of other deaths as well. Two
years after their mother's death, Stella Duckworth, who had taken on the
mother's role, died of peritonitis following an appendectomy in early
pregnancy. She was twenty-eight and had been married three months.

If Woolf thought her mother's early death was due to her
womanhood—the many births, the energy absorbed by her large family
and relentlessly demanding husband—, then how much more must
Stella's death have given her forebodings about sexuality, about

marriage, about the ability of her body to change and her inability to control that change? It was Stella who had been going "to launch [Vanessa and Virginia] out on the ordinary woman's life that promised such treasures," Stella whose engagement gave her "a standard of love; a sense that nothing in the whole world is so lyrical, so musical, as a young man and a young woman in their first love for each other." But the result of this "ruby ... glowing, red, clear, intense ... [until] [t]his colour, this incandescence, was in Stella's whole body" is her death ("A Sketch of the Past," *MB*, pp. 106, 105). While death hangs over everyone in Virginia Woolf's vision, for women there is a second sword impending. The thrust of sex is a continual threat.

At Stella's death Woolf was again motherless and left in the hands of George Duckworth, a sentimental, tyrannical, and sexually confused father figure. There was no woman to mother her into social and sexual maturity, to show her how she was and how to be. Julia Stephen's absence became as compelling as her presence had been. Her daughter writes, "Until I was in the forties— ... when I wrote *To the Lighthouse* ... —the presence of my mother obsessed me. I could hear her voice, see her, imagine what she would do or say as I went about my day's doings" ("A Sketch of the Past," *MB*, p. 80).

This obsession with the mother, this possession by the half-brother, what did they leave her of her body, her ownness? For the years 1907–1913 the closest answer we have is Rachel Vinrace in *The Voyage Out*. Hers is the story of a motherless girl suddenly taken from her amniotic world of music and sleep onto the harsh land of human relationships, sexual and imperfect. Rachel finds this land unendurable and dies at the end of the novel of "natural causes" as Stella and Thoby did. Straining for the same resolution, Woolf in 1913 tried to immerse herself in the sleep of Veronal.

Moments after he appears in *The Voyage Out*, Terence Hewet inquires "'Asleep?'" (*VO*, p. 102). Though Rachel's future fiancé is not asking about her state, she overhears him as she watches through a hotel window. Thus are introduced two motifs in the novel: an innocent voyeurism and the omnipresence of sleep. Repeatedly, the main characters observe one another through windows and Hewet tries to keep Rachel awake. Sleep is also connected to food; luncheon extinguishes "any faint flame of the human spirit"; food leads to fat, torpor, ugliness (*VO*, p. 118).

The Voyage Out is a novel about impossible barriers between people, barriers which in the end are triumphant. The most graphic example of this is the bit of tissue which constitutes Rachel's virginity. Rachel becomes engaged because she must break through her isolation into the real, or at least common, world. She dies because the engagement has committed her to a frontier she cannot cross. They had "ventured too far and exposed themselves," Helen thinks in one of her many moments of premonition (*VO*, p. 286).

To consider the barriers in *The Voyage Out* to be exclusively, or even primarily, sexual would be a mistake, however. Roger Poole has called it a novel about "the terrors of engagement" and links it with Woolf's own engagement and the sexual incompatibility of her marriage.[5] But Rachel's engagement is not only with Hewet but with the world. She has promised to enter as well as to be entered, to quit looking through windows speculating about what love and life are like. Separately and together, Rachel and Hewet find the world outside them fascinating and unreal, and this unreality encompasses their own bodies and their relationship. To marry, they must get out of the audience and join the play; in a less positive image, they must stop staring into cages and admit that they are animal. To give up possibility for actuality: this is what they have engaged to do.

But Rachel breaks this engagement with her death. She leaves the land—wakefulness, sexuality, struggle, self-exposure, community, adulthood, life—to return to the sea—sleep, sexlessness, peace, hiddenness, singularity, infancy, death. Rachel is always separated from other people by that membrane, that window, that amniotic sac, and lives in double terror lest it break, lest she be trapped in it forever. So Woolf describes the intensity of her first impressions at St. Ives, "the feeling ... of lying in a grape and seeing through a film of semi-transparent yellow" ("A Sketch of the Past," *MB*, p. 65). And she says, trying to explain to Madge Vaughan the peculiar angle of her early writing, "[M]y present feeling is that this vague & dream like world, without love, or heart, or passion, or sex, is the world I really care about, & find interesting. For, though they are dreams to you, & I cant [sic] express them at all adequately, these things are perfectly real to me" (*Letters* I, June, 1906, p. 227).

While this world "without love, or heart, or passion, or sex" may
be the one Woolf longs for, it is not the one she has known, nor can she
create and maintain it any more than Rachel can. The forces of the
world, of our own bodies, move us outward, towards intimacy, towards
change. Thus, though Woolf was originally horrified when Vanessa
claimed that they would, after all, marry, she herself married only a few
years later. And Rachel, though she is twenty-four before she
experiences so much as a kiss, becomes engaged a few months afterward.
The circumstances and results of that kiss are crucial in Rachel's story.
Richard Dalloway, lecturing her about the "opportunities and
possibilities" of life, concludes "'But about yourself?'" and she replies,
"'You see, I'm a woman.'" Even the ship lurches as the MP declares,
"'You have beauty,'" and kisses her. "'You tempt me,'" he explains in a
terrifying voice (*VO*, p. 76). In this exchange we see both that Rachel
feels herself outside the world of self-definition to which Mr. Dalloway
belongs and that he perceives her as possessing something which he
wants. In his terms the kiss is her fault because of what she is.

That night Rachel dreams of "a little deformed man ... gibbering"
with a face "like the face of an animal." Even when she wakes, she can't
escape the terror, "A voice moaned for her; eyes desired her. All night
long barbarian men harrassed the ship" (*VO*, p. 77). At the end of the
novel, when she is near death, a variant of this dream returns, but the
deformed figure is a woman, as if, during her engagement, Rachel has
transferred her horror of male sexuality onto her own.

Greater shocks follow in the wake of Dalloway's kiss. When Helen
explains that it is natural for men to want to kiss and marry her, Rachel
immediately connects this with prostitution and her lack of basic freedom:

> "So that's why I can't walk alone!"
>
> By this new light she saw her life for the first time a
> creeping hedged-in thing, driven cautiously between high
> walls, here turned aside, there plunged in darkness, made
> dull and crippled for ever—her life that was the only chance
> she had—the short season between two silences.
>
> "Because men are brutes! I hate men!" she exclaimed.
> (*VO*, p. 82)

It is this objectification of herself which Rachel cannot tolerate. She is overcome by fear and then by anger. Yet she becomes engaged to Hewet who, though an improvement over Richard Dalloway, likewise wishes to possess her, to "make ... demands," to "sit so near and keep his eye on her" and who finds her "less desirable as her brain [begins] to work" (*VO*, pp. 215, 212). He interrupts her music to read notes for his novel which assert that women "don't think" (*VO*, p. 291). He follows up this interruption by reading from a misogynist novel and then, having commanded Rachel to sit on the floor, he evaluates her appearance:

> "You're not beautiful, ... but I like your face, ... and your eyes too—they never see anything. Your mouth's too big, and your cheeks would be better if they had more colour in them. But what I like about your face is that it makes one wonder what the devil you're thinking about—it makes me want to do that—" He clenched his fist and shook it so near her that she started back, "because now you look as if you'd blow my brains out. There are moments," he continued, "when, if we stood on a rock together, you'd throw me into the sea." (*VO*, pp. 297–298)

Hewet wishes to provoke the violence in Rachel which he has told her he would feel as a woman (*VO*, p. 215). What he gets is a mock scuffle over the imaginary rock. Trying to catch her, he succeeds in knocking her to the floor where she lies "gasping, and crying for mercy." But she declares, not his triumph, but her impenetrability: "'I'm a mermaid! I can swim ... so the game's up.' Her dress was torn across" (*VO*, p. 298). The game is up because Rachel cannot live in a world where she fears being the object of Hewet's desire, fears the "little deformed man," the "horrible face ... of an animal" about which she dreams and which Virginia Woolf saw over her shoulder in the mirror at St. Ives ("A Sketch of the Past," *MB*, p. 69). As *Orlando* will explain thirteen years later:

> Love ... has two faces; one white, the other black; two bodies; one smooth, the other hairy. It has two hands, two feet, two tails, two, indeed, of every member and each one is the exact

opposite of the other. Yet, so strictly are they joined together that you cannot separate them. (*O*, p. 117)

If that hairy face connotes threat, it also signifies authority, the judge in a society where marriage and motherhood are the measuring rods of woman's stunted growth. So we find the "hairy black" image long before *Orlando*. In 1911, while at work on *The Voyage Out*, Woolf writes to Vanessa:

> Did you feel horribly depressed [over the Whitsunday holiday]? I did. I could not write, and all the devils came out—hairy black ones. To be 29 and unmarried—to be a failure—childless—insane too, no writer. (June 8?, 1911, *Letters* I, p. 466)

While Virginia Stephen claimed in regard to her sister's marriage, "I can make a living out of what is left" and "there will be all Nessa's life to look forward to," she had to have something of her own (VW to Violet Dickinson, January 3, 1907 and December 18, 1906, *Letters* I, pp. 276, 266). And though she railed at Violet Dickinson about urging her to marry, vowing to write her "such a lecture upon the carnal sins as will make you [and Kitty Maxse] fall into each others [sic] arms," (*Letters* I, p. 276), the summer of 1912 found her at the same registry office entering the same contract her sister had five years earlier.

The first autumn and spring of her marriage were strenuous, as she finished *The Voyage Out*. In July 1913, Woolf was sent for a rest cure at Twickenham. She was not well again until 1916.

If Rachel in *The Voyage Out* is a mermaid, impenetrable by nature, Clarissa Dalloway is a nun, cloistered by choice. "Fear no more the heat o' the sun," that refrain which sings in her mind all day, expresses not only her age but the shelter she has chosen, though that shelter is not entirely what she wants. The nun sacrifices her freedom and sexuality in worship of a male god. To follow the recurring image that far may seem to lose Clarissa, but in fact she *does* sacrifice herself to Richard and to the male view of women. Discontent with her appearance, guilt-ridden over "failing" Richard, uneasy about her need to impress people, aware of Peter Walsh's disapproving eye, unable to face her ties to Sally Seton and to her daughter, Clarissa is living her life according to someone else's rules, in habits that do not fit. There is a grill between her and the world, between her and herself.

Both Clarissa and her alter-ego, Septimus Warren Smith, face much the same dilemma Rachel did: how to overcome the barriers between themselves and the world without being destroyed in the process. As in the earlier novel, these barriers are often expressed as windows or, in Septimus' case, as a screen. Clarissa marvels at the barriers, calling them part of the mystery of life. "[H]ere was one room; there another. Did religion solve that, or love?" (*MD*, p. 193). Her marriage necessitates separation, which she struggles to balance by her sense of connection with the world around her:

> [H]ere, there, she survived, Peter survived, lived in each other, she being part, she was positive, of the trees at home; ... part of people she had never met; being laid out like a mist between the people she knew best, who lifted her on their branches as she had seen the trees lift the mist, but it spread ever so far, her life, herself. (*MD*, p. 12)

Septimus, on the other hand, cannot endure the barriers. Where Clarissa chides herself for lacking "something central which permeated," which "rippled the cold contact of man and woman," Septimus thinks himself condemned to death because "he did not feel" (*MD*, pp. 46, 137). Septimus' state is simply the extreme of Clarissa's: an extremity caused by society—he is a live casualty of the War—and condemned by it. Since his officer Evans' death (as since Clarissa's refusal of Peter Walsh and Sally Seton), there has been a screen over everything, a barrier which is partly death itself and partly the distance Septimus feels between himself and the world because of the vision death has brought him. The screen prevents him from delivering his urgent messages. Like Rachel, he is terrified both that the barrier is unbreachable and that it might be crossed. Like Clarissa, he feels intense connection with the world around him but the extremity of this connection is horrifying: "He would see no more" but "they beckoned; leaves were alive; trees were alive. And the leaves being connected by millions of fibres with his own body, there on the seat, fanned it up and down; when the branch stretched he, too, made that statement" (*MD*, p. 32). Because such perception is overwhelming, Septimus talks of killing himself, and the doctors close in for the cure.

Like Virginia Woolf at several points in her life, Septimus loses his autonomy. His state again is Clarissa's, is woman's; he becomes an object; his body is not his own. As Dr. Bradshaw approaches, Septimus literally has no room, so he hurls himself out the window to reality: death, Evans, Mrs. Filmer's area railings piercing him through.

Septimus' suicide—and we recall Woolf's similar attempt in 1904—enables Clarissa to accept herself and life around her, the woman going to bed across the way. His deliberate death affirms life as her party does. Her sense of herself as *subject*, creator, usually realized only in weaving the patterned moments of a party, is strengthened by Septimus' refusal to be an object. if one's self is worth throwing away to protect, it is worth owning, and "[h]ere is one room; there another" becomes a statement not of isolation but of mutual integrity, all being housed somehow together.

Septimus is not Clarissa's only counterpart in the novel. She is shadowed by Miss Kilman, who is heavy where Clarissa is delicate, coarse where she is fine, who is poor, struggling, ugly, and religious. To complete the negative, Miss Kilman has a passion for Elizabeth, the daughter Clarissa holds at arm's length. The women do not see what they have in common. Each is struggling to define herself in her own terms rather then in terms of what the (male) world wants and sees: Clarissa, unyielding object, unpossessable; Miss Kilman, ugly object, undesirable; Elizabeth, beautiful object, to be possessed.

In contrast to "the privacy of the soul" for which Septimus dies (*MD*, p. 192)—and perhaps what makes this privacy bearable in *Mrs. Dalloway* where it was not in *The Voyage Out*—is the multiplicity of connections in the larger world. Obvious ones, like the skywriting, the Prime Minister's car, the clock striking, are hallmarks of the novel. But more subtle ones are spread between the characters, like Clarissa's mist laid on the trees, and it is this which makes the parallels between Clarissa and Septimus convincing. Thoughts are handed from mind to mind as clearly as public emotions. More subtle still are the echoing perceptions: a girl in the park cries out how she shouldn't have come to London while Rezia mourns leaving Italy; Mrs. Dempster carries on Septimus' denigration of the body; Lady Bruton and Miss Kilman share the image of threads spun from their bodies as their friends leave them. This last is a personal image for Woolf, as is the screen (*WD*, pp. 98, 96, 55).

Because of this interweaving of connections, the isolation of characters in *Mrs. Dalloway* is of a different quality than that in *The Voyage Out*. Granted, there is a community drawn from hotel and villa in the early novel, but it is not communal at such depth or on so many levels. The tunnels behind characters, which Woolf describes as "my discovery" in writing *Mrs. Dalloway*, did not exist in that first work. "I dig out beautiful caves behind my characters: I think that gives exactly what I want; humanity, humour, depth. The idea is that the caves shall connect and each comes to daylight at the present moment" (*WD*, August 30, 1923, p. 59). The place where the caves connect constitutes the larger, impersonal body, not confined to male or female, age or class, which makes up the life of London on one day in June. It is the house which includes all the rooms.

Between the Acts continues the theme sounded in Mrs. *Dalloway*: a larger body of life contains individuals and its communion makes the isolation of separate bodies endurable. Woolf confirms this theme in her diary when she first thinks about the novel:

> Why not Poyntzet Hall: a centre: all literature discussed in connection with real little incongruous living humour: and anything that comes into my head; but "I" rejected: "We" substituted: to whom at the end there shall be an invocation? "We" ... waifs and strays—a rambling, capricious but somehow unified whole—the present state of my mind? (*WD*, April 26, 1938, p. 279)

Her state of mind still includes intense awareness of barriers—temperament, age, sexual attraction and estrangement—but they are to be overridden by the larger vision.

Perhaps because of her rejection of the "I" for a new subjectivity, perhaps because of inner changes which that rejection marks, Virginia Woolf has created characters in *Between the Acts* who are more believable, immediately flesh than any in her previous work. In this novel we are shown what it feels like to be old, to be middle-aged and sexually restless, to be a child exploring a luminous world.

Few of the characters are at ease in their bodies, however, and this unease is part of the tension between them. Isa feels heavy, prisoned; Giles is a farmer sewn into a city suit; Old Bart is acutely aware of his frail veins; William Dodge labels himself "a half-man" (*BA*, p. 73). One of the novel's rare instances of real communication occurs when Mrs. Swithin and William, an old woman and a homosexual, look in a mirror together. "Cut off from their bodies, their eyes smile[]" (*BA*, p. 71). Likewise, William and Isa can talk because there is no sexual tension between them.

Mrs. Swithin with her religion, Miss La Trobe with her art, Mrs. Manresa with her luxuriant sensuality: these three seem to move beyond the prison of their women's bodies toward some autonomy. But Mrs. Swithin is called Old Flimsy and Batty by the young people and ridiculed by her brother; Miss La Trobe is labelled Bossy, an outsider because of appearance, profession, and sexual preference; and Mrs. Manresa appears to act as *subject* only because she takes the lead in defining herself as *object*. She is the "wild child," the "natural woman" that some men delight in, created and maimed as it is for their pleasure. Old Bart reflects that Isa, whose mind is "up in the clouds, like an air ball" may lack the body to hold his son down, but Mrs. Manresa is another story. "Giles [will] keep his orbit so long as she weight[s] him to the earth" (*BA*, pp. 116, 119). Isa writes poetry, hidden, like herself. Mrs. Manresa reeks sex. Giles despises them both.

When Miss La Trobe's actors hold up mirrors to the audience creating "Present Time. Ourselves," only Mrs. Manresa is unruffled. The others squirm and are offended at this sudden encounter with their bodies, this vision of forms which do not embody them as they know themselves, but are all that the world has to go on. Woolf has learned that she does not face that horror alone.

The artist, Miss La Trobe, literally holds the mirror up to nature in *Between the Acts* and, in the end, is seen writing the life beyond the book. Giles and Isa, about to speak to each other for the first time as we leave them, are the characters in Miss La Trobe's new play. On her they depend just as she is a "slave" to them, to her audience (*BA*, p. 94). She recognizes her slavery as the play is being performed, and her insight, taken with the end of the novel, reveals the most intricate form of interdependence Virginia Woolf knows: the network by which we create and recreate one another.

But finally the community of spirit—past and present, living and dead (Orlando's house, Mrs. Dalloway's London)—in *Between the Acts* cannot transcend the individual's isolation and paralysis because the community itself, on the brink of World War II, is isolated and paralysed. The description of the audience at the Pageant covers also their state of mind as they wait, helpless spectators, for the last act of civilization: "All their nerves were on edge. They sat exposed. The machine ticked .... They were suspended, without being, in limbo. Tick, tick, tick went the machine" (*BA*, p. 178). While Giles and Miss La Trobe are most conscious of the threat, other characters feel the sword over their heads. Isa mutters:

> "Four and twenty blackbirds, strung upon a string, ...
> Down came an Ostrich, an eagle, an executioner,
> 'Which of you is ripe,' he said, 'to bake in my pie?
> Which of you is ripe, which of you is ready,
> Come my pretty gentleman,
> Come my pretty lady.' ... "
>
> (*BA*, p. 178)

So when Woolf writes in her diary, "I can't conceive that there will be a June 27, 1941," Isa says of the Pageant, "'This year, last year, next year, never'" (*WD*, June 22, 1940, p. 325; *BA*, p. 217).

By the time Virginia Woolf is writing the second half of *Between the Acts*, it is clear to her that the *We* she so gallantly hoped to write as, to speak for, is as threatened as the old I, that in fact civilization—history, literature, other, self—is disintegrating. The *We* has become "a gnat on a blade of grass" and "the writing 'I' has vanished" (*WD*, August 17, 1938, p. 290; June 9, 1940, p. 323).

In retrospect, we see that the novel's title refers not only to its tenure "between the acts" of two world wars, the acts of Miss La Trobe's play (both the Pageant and the one which Giles and Isa are living), and the sexual acts of their marriage, but to the circumstances of its creation. For it is written between the acts of living and dying; it is a testament of the last will, the artist clearing the way for what she can scarcely believe will go on beyond her: spoken words, written words, laboring "to put the severed parts together," to make "of the moment something permanent," of the mortal body something that lasts ("A Sketch of the Past," *MB*, p. 72; *TL*, p. 241). In the closing words of *Between the Acts*, she sets the stage even as she leaves it: "Then the curtain rose. They spoke" (*BA*, p. 219).

In "Professions for Women" Woolf states, "[T]elling the truth about my own experiences as a body [is a problem] I do not think I solved. I doubt that any woman has solved it yet" ("Professions for Women," *DM*, p. 241). Barriers to writing about her body include her sense of body itself as barrier, both prisoning and protecting the self. That she perceived the body as an excess of the spirit is evident in diary entries about her own writing: "I ... determined to sweat [*The Pargiters*] bare of flesh before going on," and "To get to the bones, now I'm writing fiction again I feel my force glow straight from me at its fullest" (*WD*, August 24, 1933, p. 204; *WD*, June 19, 1923, p. 56). Woolf wishes to be unaware of her sex when writing fiction because the sense of oppression and anger which come with that awareness disrupts the unconscious state of the novelist ("Professions for Women," *DM*, p. 239). In *A Room of One's Own* she warns that "[i]t is fatal for a woman to lay the least stress on any grievance; to plead even with justice any cause; in any way to speak consciously as a woman" (p. 181). That Woolf herself does not always heed this warning is clear (see *The Pargiters*, *The Years*, Michele Barrett's introduction to *Women and Writing*[6]), but that is her intention. To be *subject*, she seems to say, I have had to minimize my body, to govern and interpret its sensations, to set it apart, inviolable, a room of my own. Surely this is as much due to the forced surrender of her autonomy during mental breakdowns as to her determination to survive as a woman and write. But the two skeins are woven together so tightly and elaborately that we cannot say what is background and what is pattern, what results from such mental distress and what fashions it. And we must remember that we are speaking of a whole person, a continuous life, not of a Genius whose writing table was turned over at certain intervals by Madness and who was rendered Other until the Madness passed.

There is a point in *The Great Gatsby* when Nick describes his hero on the verge of kissing Daisy and thus touching the face of his dream. The assumptions on which this description rests are the barriers that Woolf or any woman faces in the effort to become the *subject*, to live from the inside out: "He knew that when he kissed this girl, and forever wed his unutterable visions to her perishable breath, his mind would never romp again like the mind of God."[7] The premises are so ingrained and the prose so seductive that at first their message may slip in unperceived: if it weren't for women, men would be immortal; women do not have "unutterable thoughts" or minds that want to "romp ... like the mind of God." They want only to capture such a mind, to weight it down, like Mrs. Manresa, and make from it a bloody issue. No wonder Virginia Woolf turned her back on this deadly arrangement; no wonder she thought herself "an outsider" and grew surer in the last years of the need to revise life and fiction, to "take [her] own way" (*WD*, May 20, 1938, p. 282).

NOTES

1. Adrienne Rich, *Of Woman Born* (New York: Norton, 1976), p. 284.

2. Rich, p. 284.

3. For the classic treatment of the split between subject and object, see Simone de Beauvoir, *The Second Sex*, trans. and ed. H. M. Parshley (1949; rpt. New York: Bantam, 1961), pp. 43–47, 676ff.

4. James Naremore, *The World Without a Self: Virginia Woolf and the Novel* (New Haven: Yale University Press, 1973).

5. Roger Poole, *The Unknown Virginia Woolf* (Cambridge: Cambridge University Press, 1978), Chapter 3, pp. 33–53. While Poole's book lacks balance, I am indebted to his analysis of the extent to which Septimus Warren Smith is autobiographical.

6. *Women and Writing*, ed. and with an introduction by Michele Barrett (New York: Harcourt, 1979).

7. F. Scott Fitzgerald, *The Great Gatsby* (1925; rpt. New York: Scribner's, 1953), p. 112.

CHRISTOPHER REED

Through Formalism: Feminism and Virginia Woolf's Relation to Bloomsbury Aesthetics

Over the last forty years, literature scholars have been turning to art history, investigating the aesthetic doctrines of formalism developed within the Bloomsbury group in order to understand their effect on the writing of Virginia Woolf.[1] At this point, it seems only fair that the tables be turned and an art historian look to Woolf's writings for insight into formalism. That such a critical inquiry should only now suggest itself indicates not its lack of importance, but, on the contrary, the strength of formalism's hold over the unquestioned assumptions of art historical practice. Like Keynesian economics, Bloomsbury's formalist aesthetic theory extended its influence far beyond the immediate circle in which it developed. Throughout the English-speaking world, the writings of Roger Fry and Clive Bell opened the way for the creation and reception of modern art in the first decades of this century.

The rejection of mimesis and concentration on the play of abstract form: these were the fundamental tenets of Bloomsbury's aesthetic theory. As the center of the art world shifted from Europe to the United States after World War II, these principles were absorbed by American critics—foremost among them Clement Greenberg—and became the basis for modernist creative and critical practice. Only recently, in the culture of "postmodernism," has there been any broad movement in art scholarship to question formalism's philosophical premises or to see its rise to preeminence as anything but inevitable. As we assess the strengths and the weaknesses of a philosophy that in its maturity came to dominate our field so completely, we become curious about the historical conditions of its birth, and specifically about the reactions of those who may be said to have attended its delivery and participated in its early development.

As one of the keenest and most articulate members of the Bloomsbury group, Virginia Woolf's reactions to emergent formalism are naturally important. Woolf's take on formalism is of special interest, however, because her consistently insightful feminism anticipates a crucial component in the current postmodernist rejection of formalism. Feminist artists and critics have challenged Greenbergian formalism's claim to transcend all extra-aesthetic concerns. They have revealed, behind its professed objectivity, an ideology strongly marked by patriarchal values: a penchant for hierarchization and the assumption of unchallengeable authority among critics, a model of isolated and antisocial creativity for artists, and a bias toward art that emphasizes size and brawn—huge raw metal sculptures, for example, or house paint flung upon great swatches of canvas.[2] That this later generation of formalists should generally characterize Woolf as a second-rate Joyce and dismiss the community of Bloomsbury painters altogether reveals the depth of the rupture between formalism's initial conception in Bloomsbury and its later deployment.[3]

Woolf's initial reaction of skepticism and continuing ambivalence toward formalism suggests that problematic assumptions about critical authority, creativity, and art's social role beset formalism from its inception. Still, the undisputed importance of formalist theory for Woolf and her lasting devotion to its progenitor, Roger Fry, stand as testimony that as an aesthetic system formalism is not without its appeal. In short, Virginia Woolf found herself sixty years ago in a position of ambivalence similar to that of many of us today. The account of her relationship to formalism contributes both to the history of twentieth-century thought and to contemporary debates over aesthetics.

My introduction suggests that a chronological approach to the study of Woolf and formalism is not simply the reflex of art scholarship, which—despite its similarities to literary criticism—is a branch of history, and so tends to emphasize chronology. As a historian, I believe that our current understanding of the relationship between Woolf and formalism has suffered from a tendency to read the relevant texts without regard to their dates of issue, imposing a false stasis on what reveals itself as, actually, a remarkably dynamic relationship. It is significant, for example, that Woolf did not find formalism immediately and self-evidently useful. One reason, certainly, is that in its first phase, between 1909 and 1917, formalism explicitly opposed itself to literature. Even the term "literary" applied to art signified an unhealthy emphasis on illusion at the expense of such formal values identified by Fry as rhythm of line, mass, proportion, light and shade, color, and perspective.[4] In 1914, Clive Bell's *Art*, a summary of formalist principles developed primarily by Fry in journalistic essays published over the previous few years, concluded that because art is sullied by any reference outside itself, "Literature is never pure art .... Most of it is concerned, to some extent, with facts and ideas." At about the same time, Roger Fry was writing, "I think literature is usually very little to do with art,"[5] and Woolf later recalled the prescriptions for literature he made at this time: "He laid sacrilegious hands upon the classics. He found glaring examples in Shakespeare, in Shelley, of the writer's vice of ... importing impure associations .... Literature was suffering from a plethora of old clothes. Cézanne and Picasso had shown the way; writers should fling representation to the winds and follow suit" (*RF* 172).

For her part, Woolf at this period remarked of her Bloomsbury colleagues and their penchant for purely formal values, "[A]rtists are an abominable race. The furious excitement of these people all the winter, over their pieces of canvas coloured green and blue is odious" (*L* 2:15). Her early fiction—both *The Voyage Out* (1915) and *Night and Day* (1919)—is characterized by the conspicuous rejection of formalism. In the first, it comes when Terence reads Milton aloud, "because he said the words of Milton had substance and shape, so that it was not necessary to understand what he was saying" (*VO* 326). This insistence that pure aesthetic experience is contaminated by any signification marks Terence as a convert to the early formalism codified in *Art*. Woolf recounts, however, that, "The words, in spite of what Terence had said, seemed to be laden with meaning, and perhaps it was for this reason that it was painful to listen to them" (*VO* 326). Even David Dowling, a critic who is so determined to ground Woolf's fiction in Fry's aesthetic theory that he cites the descriptive passages in *The Voyage Out* as examples of "painterly vision" (whatever that may mean—certainly not the purely abstract art the Bloomsbury artists were producing at the time), ultimately has to acknowledge that during the period of its composition, "Woolf felt that the painter was engaged essentially in a different task from the novelist."[6]

Formalist aesthetics are more explicitly at issue in *Night and Day*, which Woolf began in 1916. Here art seen in the formalist manner as "a glow of faintly pleasing pink and brown tints" stultifies the heroine, putting her in "a pleasant dreamy state" (*ND* 319, 16), and it is only when Katharine uses the portrait of her grandfather to imagine him as "a man, young, unhappy, tempestuous, full of desires and faults," that she escapes the weight of convention and is able to make her ancestor an ally in change. Now, "doubts, questionings, and despondencies she felt, as she looked up, would be more welcome to him than homage" (*ND* 320). Even Ralph Denham's expressive doodle, a "little dot with ... flames round it," functions mimetically as "it represented ... all that encircling glow which for him surrounded, inexplicably, so many of the objects of life" (*ND* 493). Most revealing is Woolf's slyly dismissive use of formalism's vocabulary of "aesthetic emotion" when Mary Datchet goes to see the marbles in the British Museum: "One must suppose, at least, that her emotions were not purely esthetic, because, after she had gazed at the Ulysses for a minute or two, she began to think about Ralph Denham" (*ND* 82). Mary goes on, in a most unformalist way, to invent fantastical stories in response to the images before her.

Yet only a few years after this evocation of art as little more than an effective impetus to storytelling—an attitude she humorously notes would mean the loss "of my aesthetic soul" in the eyes of her formalist friends (*D* 1:168)[7]—Woolf found herself prepared to assert the dependence of modern literature on painting. In 1925, she wrote:

> [W]e are under the dominion of painting. Were all modern paintings to be destroyed, a critic of the twenty-fifth century would be able to deduce from the works of Proust alone the existence of Matisse, Cézanne, Derain, and Picasso; he would be able to say with those books before him that painters of the highest originality and power must be covering canvas after canvas, squeezing tube after tube, in the room next door. ("Pictures," 173)

What had transpired since Woolf's first exposure to formalist theory was a change, not only in Woolf, but also in formalism.

The constantly evolving quality of Bloomsbury formalism is largely ignored in histories of aesthetics that measure the accomplishments of Fry and Bell in terms of their usefulness to the next generation of Americans. This is not the place for a thorough exegesis of the development of Bloomsbury formalism after the initial single-minded emphasis on abstract form epitomized by Clive Bell's *Art*. If the basic aim of Bloomsbury's later aesthetic theorizing can be encapsulated, however, it is the attempt to reintegrate representation into the formalist paradigm without sacrificing an ideal of purely aesthetic experience. The shift from first- to second-generation formalism in Bloomsbury may be marked from around the end of World War I. By 1917, Clive Bell and others were complaining of Fry's waning interest in avant-garde art,[8] and it was around this time that Fry became interested in the aesthetics of poetry and began what would become a lifelong project translating Mallarmé.

Having opened itself to issues of language and representation, formalism in its second incarnation began to attract Woolf's interest.[9] As early as 1916, she crowed: "I predict the complete rout of post impressionism, chiefly because Roger, who has been staying with us, is now turning to literature, and says pictures only do 'to look at about 4 times'" (*L* 2:77–78). In diary entries of November 1917, she moves rapidly from "I don't like talking art in front of him" (*D* 1:75) to "taking a splendid flight above personalities, we discussed literature & aesthetics" (*D* 1:80).[10] Woolf here quotes Fry's contribution to the discussion: "[A]ll art is representative. You say the word tree, & you see a tree. Very well. Now every word has an aura. Poetry combines the different auras in a sequence." This may be taken as the first record of a theory Fry repeated in a draft of the introduction to his Mallarmé translation, where he rejected poetry without signification as having negligible aesthetic effect. Fry ultimately published his thesis in *Transformations*: "There is [in poetry] the pleasure of rhythmic utterance, but this is already concerned with relations, and even this is, I believe, accessory to the emotion aroused by rhythmic changes of states of mind due to the meanings of the words."[11]

Fry's partner in developing the second phase of formalist theory was not Clive Bell, who had joined him in the first, but the young

French intellectual Charles Mauron. Like Fry, Mauron was trained as a scientist, a career he was forced to leave due to failing sight. After their meeting in 1919, Fry encouraged Mauron to turn his attention to literature, which he did, eventually inventing the critical technique of "psychocritique." By 1925, Fry was publishing Mauron's articles on aesthetics in the *Burlington Magazine* and together they addressed the Décades de Pointigny conference, with Fry reporting of Mauron's paper: "It clears up endless points and completes my aesthetic." In 1927, the Woolfs' Hogarth Press published Mauron's *Burlington Magazine* essays and the address from the Décades conference, translated by Fry and combined under the title *The Nature of Beauty in Art and Literature*. Its stated purpose was to resolve "the old scholastic distinction of form and content." To this end, Mauron proposed the solidification of Fry's "auras" into "psychological volumes" as the "analog" to the physical volumes manipulated by the visual artist: "As the painter creates a spatial being, the writer creates a psychological being."[12] Woolf may have put it more eloquently when, in 1925, she described how Proust illuminated "the hard tangible material shapes of bodiless thoughts" ("Pictures," 175). The year before, she had written to an old friend, the painter Jacques Raverat, suggesting that the writer's art is "to catch and consolidate ... those splashes of yours" (*L* 3:135), and as early as 1918, she was asserting her "plastic sense of words" (*D* 1:168). However the phrasing varies, it is clear that Woolf was very much in the thick of Bloomsbury's aesthetic theorizing in the years after World War I.

It is not my purpose here to repeat the detailed exegeses of formalism's influence on Woolf's postwar fiction (cited in note 1). Neither am I proposing complete "readings" of the novels under discussion. Rather, I am looking at how Woolf's writing illuminates both the attractions and dangers of formalist practice. Because of feminism's active hand in the undermining of formalist authority, there has been a tendency for critics to assume that the two philosophies are inherently at odds.[13] Given the feminist consciousness clearly in evidence from her earliest writings, however, it would be surprising if Woolf's subsequent attraction to formalism were unaffected by her feminism, and, in fact, Woolf as early as 1919 can be found deploying formalist principles in support of feminist arguments. In "Modern Novels" (a review in *The Times Literary Supplement* slightly revised and republished as "Modern Fiction"), Woolf adopts the language of formalism as part of a feminist strategy to gain authority over "Mr. Wells, Mr. Bennett, and Mr. Galsworthy." Using the formalist valorization of aesthetic purity, Woolf is able to transcend conventional critical hierarchies that would privilege the treatment of subjects deemed significant by the dominant (patriarchal) culture. As a formalist, she can turn the tables on what had seemed the high moral stance of her triumvirate of male authors, dismissing what she calls the materialism of their writing as "immense skill and immense industry making the trivial and the transitory appear the true and the enduring" (*CE* 2:105).[14] In a later version of this argument, Woolf ties her critique of Wells, Bennett, and Galsworthy to her condemnation of those who would betray what she calls "the *form* of the novel" by using it "to preach doctrines, sing songs, or celebrate the glories of the British Empire" (*CE* 1:324; my emphasis). And Woolf came to ground her reversal of standard literary values explicitly in a feminist sensibility: "When a woman comes to write a novel, she will find that she is perpetually wishing to alter the established values—to make serious what appears insignificant to a man, and trivial what is to him important" (*CE* 2:146). This explicitly feminist argument reveals the ideology inherent in Woolf's admonition in "Modern Fiction" that novelists reject the dictates of convention, which she personifies as "some powerful and unscrupulous tyrant" who insists on "plot" (*CE* 2:106). Instead, Woolf argues, novelists should look for formal significance in the traditionally feminine realm of the everyday, what she calls "the life of Monday or Tuesday," a phrase that, not coincidentally, reappears as the title of her first book of short stories: "Examine for a moment an ordinary mind on an ordinary day .... Let us record the atoms as they fall upon the mind in the order in which they fall, let us trace the pattern .... Let us not take it for granted that life exists more fully in what is commonly thought big than in what is commonly thought small" (*CE* 2:106–7). The claims of pattern here support a vehement rejection of the literary tradition of Bennett, Wells, and Galsworthy: "the sooner English fiction turns its back upon them ... the better for its soul" (*CE* 2:104).[15]

Even more provocative in Woolf's appreciation of formalism's potential feminist application is her emphasis on its disruption of assumptions about the nature of aesthetic experience. From the very earliest references to art—Zeuxis's grapes so real the birds pecked at them, Pygmalion's vivification of Galatea, Apelles' acquisition of

Campaspe through his art—representation in western culture has been profoundly implicated in networks of desire and possession, so that by 1908, when Freud succinctly assessed the cultural role of art as fantasy fulfillment, he enumerated two categories of its appeal. Art, Freud says, affords its producers and consumers with vicarious access to what they cannot in real life attain, "wishes" for authority and sexual gratification. It is exactly this paradigm that Woolf attacks when she castigates the pictures exhibited at the Royal Academy, which were designed "to radiate the strange power to make the beholder more heroic and more romantic" (*CE* 4:210). But this phrase is, itself, a rewriting of a sentence from Clive Bell's *Art*, where he remarks that representational art merely "afford[s] new points of departure for new trains of romantic feeling or heroic thought."[16]

Feminist scholarship has done a great deal to specify the pernicious effect of romance and heroism on the depiction of women in patriarchal culture and the constitution of viewership as a form of authority.[17] Formalists, in their insistence that art be valued purely for its intrinsic aesthetic qualities, early on opposed conventions that used art as this kind of access to its subject matter. Mauron admonished: "The mistake is to suppose that there is a subject and a work which represents it. There is no subject, there are only objects which may have served as models ... and there is beside, independent, real and different, this work itself." Nor did the first formalists shirk the gendered implications of their arguments. Fry went before a conference of psychoanalysts to reiterate the principle—asserted since his "Essay in Aesthetics" of 1909—that true art functions only in relation to a "detached" or "disinterested" vision that takes no part in desire. Examples of non-art, Fry told the psychoanalysts, are the pictures of "a beautiful woman" that appeal to "qualities which have nothing, or almost nothing, to do with their formal design or their aesthetic quality in the strict sense."[18] Here, he is repeating a point Clive Bell made in *Art*, where the difference between desire and aesthetic emotion is emphasized because, Bell says, the two are widely confused:

> With the man-in-the-street "beautiful" is more often than not synonymous with "desirable"; the word does not necessarily connote any aesthetic reaction whatever, and I am tempted to believe that in the minds of many the sexual

flavor of the word is stronger than the aesthetic. I have noticed a consistency in those to whom the most beautiful thing in the world is a beautiful woman, and the next most beautiful thing a picture of one.[19]

In the formalists' insistence on "disinterested" looking is a rudimentary attempt to problematize seeing as vicarious possession, art that would serve desire.

For Bloomsbury's formalist art critics, the injunction to disinterested contemplation translated, in practice, to an injunction against simple mimesis, a judgment shared by Woolf in the mid-1920s, her period of strongest commitment to formalism. In a 1925 essay, Woolf insisted that painters not contaminate their art with "story-telling," but "say what they have to say by shading greens into blues, posing block upon block." Such pure art, Woolf says, inspires her writing: "Cézanne, for example—no painter is more provocative to the literary sense, because his pictures are so audaciously and provocatively content to be paint that the very pigment, [writers] say, seems to challenge us, to press on some nerve, to stimulate, to excite" ("Pictures," 175–76). How to apply the injunction against mimesis to prose and escape the model of art as vicarious access to experience otherwise denied became a driving force behind the innovations in Woolf's novels of this time.

Begun the day after "hearing Roger discourse" on an exhibition of African carvings ("I dimly see that something in their style might be written" [*L* 2:429]), *Jacob's Room* (1922) starts with the author describing Jacob's mother while an artist paints her. From the opening words, which Mrs. Flanders writes and then smudges like the "hasty violet-black dab" with which she herself is rendered (*JR* 8), Woolf's technique is to mediate the narrative through layers of representation that deny traditional authorial claims to an omniscient knowledge transferable to the reader. Here the painter's rejection of seeing-as-having is translated into the author's refusal to give authoritative knowledge. We are left at the end of *Jacob's Room* unable to *know* or *comprehend* its central figure—and it is significant that both terms carry a double sense of intellectual understanding and physical possession or inclusion, a dynamic underlined in the narrative, as Jacob evades all attempts to understand or embrace him.

Woolf's narrative technique—as well as its trope, the painter in the text—is pushed to what has been widely judged a more successful level in her *To the Lighthouse* (1927). Here Lily Briscoe's struggle to complete her painting of Mrs. Ramsay parallels, from beginning to end, the authorial project of a novel in which Woolf refuses to fulfill the narrator's traditional function. As Erich Auerbach puts it in *Mimesis*: "The writer as narrator of objective facts has almost completely vanished; ... we are not given the objective information which Virginia Woolf possesses regarding these objects of her creative imagination." The language of Auerbach's description is instructive in its demonstration of the critic's contest with an author who refuses him the conventional reader's (or viewer's) position of voyeuristic privilege. Auerbach's struggle with Woolf is fascinating in that he does not overtly oppose her stance; on the contrary, his essay on *To the Lighthouse* appears as the celebratory conclusion to his survey of Western literature. Yet his frustration is clear in the phrasing, "We are not taken into Virginia Woolf's confidence and allowed to share her knowledge of Mrs. Ramsay's character," or again in his remark that Woolf "does not seem to bear in mind that she is the author and hence ought to know how matters stand with her characters." Just as Auerbach unselfconsciously wields a patriarchal standard to brand the domestic episodes of the novel "minor, unimpressive, random events," his resistance to Woolf's text is startlingly demonstrated by his quotation and then virtual rewriting of several pages of her narrative so that it makes sense "systematically." The gendered implications of Auerbach's struggle with Woolf's writing become explicit only in his last paragraphs, where he asserts that *To the Lighthouse* is filled "with good and genuine love but also, in its feminine way, with irony, amorphous sadness, and doubt of life." Almost immediately after identifying the text as feminine, however, Auerbach insists that he can know it, indeed possess it as if it were his own life: "What takes place here ... concerns the elementary things which men in general have in common."[20] Auerbach's bluster seeks to mask the critic's frustration Woolf describes in *A Room of One's Own* in the face of texts that fracture convention by being ordered "as a woman would, if she wrote like a woman." That the order being subverted is one that confers on the reader an ersatz authority is evident in Woolf's tongue-in-cheek complaint—which might be a parody of Auerbach's critical style: "[T]hus [the woman author] made it impossible for me to roll out my sonorous phrases about 'elemental feelings,' the 'common stuff of humanity,' 'depths of the human heart,' and all those other phrases which support us in our belief that, however clever we may be on top, we are very serious, very profound and very humane underneath" (*AROO* 95).

Auerbach's desire to know *To the Lighthouse*—to comprehend its "feminine" mystery into the world of "men"—marks his distance from Bloomsbury's formalism. Mauron had instructed his readers to "listen long, be sincere, and not believe too surely that one will understand." The ability to resist being known, in fact, Mauron made the definitive quality of a work of art: "As soon, then, as a phenomenon becomes sufficiently complex to be incomprehensible, it enters into the domain where a work of art becomes possible."[21] In contrast, Woolf tied the "rough and ready" move to comprehend explicitly to patriarchal privilege. She recalled how her brother Thoby "had consumed Shakespeare, somehow or other, by himself. He had possessed himself of it in his large clumsy way," which allowed him to dismiss as "sentimental" those aspects of the playwright's work that did not suit his purposes, and use the rest to buttress his own authority: "Shakespeare was to him his other world ... where he ... took his bearings." Thoby, Woolf said, was able to use Shakespeare to reinforce his masculine confidence as one "unperturbed, equipped; as if placing it all. I felt ... that he knew his own place; and relished his inheritance; I felt he ... was already, in anticipation, a law maker; proud of his station as a man; ready to play his part among men" (*MB* 138–39).

Patricia Joplin has described how Auerbach's insistence on knowing *To the Lighthouse* reveals the unlearning of a lesson learned in Woolf's novel by the painter: "The anxious desire for an author who knows (possesses) her characters and who should share that knowledge of them with us, her readers, is akin to Lily Briscoe's arousal and frustration by her subject and model .... [S]o long as Lily shares Auerbach's desire for a certain kind of knowledge of Mrs. Ramsay, she cannot complete her painting."[22] It is a disinterested, purely aesthetic gaze that in *To the Lighthouse* Lily must learn for herself, once having observed it in Mr. Bankes's gaze of love, "that never attempted to clutch its object; but, like the love which mathematicians bear their symbols, or poets their phrases, was meant to be spread over the world and become part of the human gain" (*TTL* 73–74). Here Woolf's prose echoes Clive Bell's description of "aesthetic emotion," which is like the experience of "the pure mathematician rapt in his studies."[23] When Lily finishes her painting—and Woolf ends her text—with the realization "I have had my vision," it is an acknowledgment that what neither they nor the reader have *had* is Mrs. Ramsay.

To the Lighthouse is Woolf's most eloquent investigation of the connections between formalism and feminism. The painting Lily Briscoe struggles over is expressly opposed to the predictable "pink women on the beach" painted by the contented men amid a swarm of admiring little boys (*TTL* 23) and is connected to her refusal to marry or play a traditionally feminine role. Making its focus the stable pyramid of a woman and child framed in the window of a house, her picture fulfills Woolf's belief in a woman's art that renders important what had been considered insignificant. But Lily does not simply replace one subject with another. She simplifies, abstracts, and adjusts her image until it attains the independence from its model that makes it neither a substitute for the unattainable Mrs. Ramsay nor a symbol of "universal veneration," but significant in itself as an arrangement of form (*TTL* 81–83). After the publication of *To the Lighthouse*, Woolf wrote to Fry, refusing as "hateful" any attempt to read universal symbolism in her text, and saying she wished she had dedicated the book to him, for "you have ... kept me on the right path, so far as writing goes, more than anyone" (*L* 3:385).[24]

Woolf's path to the formalism of *To the Lighthouse* was not, however, free of pitfalls; nor did she always afterwards see art in formalist terms. Early on, she stumbled into one of the fundamental dilemmas of formalism: its unresolved contradiction between two models of artistic creation, *finding* and *making*. Even within the same text, Bloomsbury formalism may often be found wavering between claiming, on the one hand, that artists *find* "significant form"—be it visual or psychological volume—in the real world and instinctively record it, and, on the other hand, that significant form is *made* by artists, becoming a testament to talent and an embodiment of individual personality. As a philosophy of art, formalism's primary concern was always the development of a theory of aesthetic response rather than artistic creation, and Fry was content to dismiss the problem with the rather vague conclusion that "In most artists we find these two impulses present in various degrees, and sometimes they vary in relative intensity at different periods."[25] Woolf falls solidly into the dilemma when, in the opening lines of the 1924 "Mr. Bennett and Mrs. Brown," she states: "My belief [is] that men and women write novels because they are lured on to create some character which has thus imposed itself upon them" (*CE* 1:319). A conscious creation or an ineluctable imposition by some preexisting entity? Woolf, like her formalist brethren, here asserts her right to decide not to decide.

The stories published together as *Monday or Tuesday* (1921), however, suggest that Woolf's entry into formalism was marked by considerable anxiety concerning standards of reality and authorial control. The "varieties of narrative voice" in *Monday or Tuesday* have been noticed before.[26] "The String Quartet" follows a model of author as finder, presenting snatches of conversation, thought, visual images, as if simply transcribed. This model is pushed to an extreme in "Blue & Green"—the colors in the title are those Woolf associated with painting (*TTL* 309; "Pictures," 175; *L* 2:15)—in which two short scenes and their associations are described. "The Mark on the Wall," at the other extreme, takes as its nominal subject something so tiny that the story becomes explicitly the chronicle of the writer's conscious thought. Despite the "solution" of the last line, giving the mark its identity, the focus is far more on the narrator (she is not "a very vigilant housekeeper," not at all interested in "historical fiction," "can think sitting still as well as standing up,") than on the snail (*CSF* 84–85, 87). It is, however, especially in "An Unwritten Novel"—where the novel's status as "unwritten" is significant of an authorial crisis—that the dilemma is explicit. Its narrator creates a story out of an incident witnessed in the world (an incident remarkably like the one still bothering Woolf in "Mr. Bennett and Mrs. Brown"), only to find that the world undermines the "truth" of her tale. Woolf's authorial voice here becomes explicitly a painter's, as she debates whether to throw in a bunch of rhododendrons for their "fling of red and white," or admonishes her central character: "Indeed now you can't sit praying any longer. Kruger's sunk beneath the clouds—washed over as with a painter's brush of liquid grey, to which he adds a tinge of black ... " (*CSF* 118, 116). The final paragraphs lurch desperately from pride of comprehension ("I've read you right—I'm with you now") to despair ("What do I stand on? What do I know?") and finally to a determination to celebrate the contradiction: "it's you, unknown figures, you I adore; if I open my arms, it's you I embrace" (*CSF* 121). This resolution to embrace what nevertheless remains unknown, depicting without possessing, anticipates Lily's attitude in *To the Lighthouse*: "And this, Lily thought, taking the green paint on her brush, this making up scenes about them, is what we call 'knowing' people ... ! Not a word of it was true; she had made it up; but it was what she knew them by all the same. She went on tunnelling her way into her picture, into the past" (*TTL* 258).

More troubling than this initial ambivalence over the formalist author's relationship to her text, however, what finally undermined Woolf's allegiance to formalism concerned its insistence on the aesthetic as a realm completely apart from other experience. I have dwelt on the potential of this position to release art from the confines of patriarchal fantasy fulfillment. There is, however, an attendant sacrifice on two fronts. First is the loss, attendant on dismissing as irrelevant the old conventions of mimetic accuracy, of all but the most solipsistic critical criteria—a dilemma, Woolf notes, for the writer no less than the critic (*CE* 2:181). The significance of "significant form" lies finally in the eye of the beholder, and despite its retention of an earlier vocabulary that assessed good art as more "real," Bloomsbury could never justify its judgments beyond subjective assertions of harmony, balance, and right relations. Woolf does not escape this confusion. In "Mr. Bennett and Mrs. Brown" she praises "real" characters, but "real" she says does not mean "lifelike," leading her to wonder "who are the judges of reality?" (*CE* 1:325). Her review of E. M. Forster's *Aspects of the Novel*, which appeared in the same year as *To the Lighthouse*, criticized his recourse to "life" as a criterion of judgment: "What is this 'Life' that keeps on cropping up so mysteriously ... in books about fiction? Why is it absent in a pattern and present in a tea party?" (*CE* 2:53). But Woolf despaired of finding an arbiter of literary pattern who could "take a stick and point to that tone, that relation, in the vanishing pages, as Mr. Roger Fry points with his wand at a line or a colour in the picture displayed before him" (*CE* 2: 54). Woolf's complaint, however, invites the question of what qualified Fry as the arbiter of visual pattern, a crisis of critical authority that Bloomsbury countered by asserting the subjectivity of all aesthetic experience, and hence all aesthetic judgment,[27] while at the same time making a somewhat contradictory appeal to inborn "taste."

Unfortunately, it was this latter claim to authoritative critical taste that was taken up in Greenbergian formalism and now prompts postmodernist attacks on Bloomsbury's "aesthetic eugenics."[28] Such criticism, however justified, ignores the importance of the other voice in Bloomsbury formalism, which, increasingly in the period after World War I, led to an engaging problematization of critical authority and the acceptance of individual variations of aesthetic response.[29] Woolf's biography of Fry makes much of the variability in his critical judgment, quoting him as saying, "I no longer think that there is a right way or a wrong way of painting ... every way is right when it is expressive throughout of the idea in the artist's mind" (*RF* 250). In a late essay, "The Leaning Tower," Woolf translates this relativism into advice for how prospective authors should read, not a limited catalog of masterpieces, but "omniverously, simultaneously, poems, plays, novels, histories, biographies, the old and the new ... ; each of us has an appetite that must find for itself the food that nourishes it" (*CE* 2:181).

If the loss of absolute criteria for the creation and criticism of art could be relatively easily absorbed into a broader ideology of relativism, however, the second sacrifice entailed by belief in the integrity of pure aesthetics turned out to be harder to live with. It involved the resignation of art's claim to social relevance. Although Fry and Bell embraced this conclusion during the heady days of early formalism in the teens, the trade-off continued to trouble Woolf, especially during the worsening political climate of the thirties.[30] Recent scholarship has illuminated the passionate engagement in social issues that characterizes Woolf's writing at this period, marking its distance from her earlier formalist exhortations that "writing must be formal," and "books will be deformed and twisted" if the author "will write in a rage where she should write calmly" (*D* 2:321; *AROO* 72–73). Her struggle to bring art and politics together is most poignantly recorded in her abortive "novel-essay" *The Pargiters*, which she eventually split into *The Years* (1937) and *Three Guineas* (1938).

Despite her failure to unite the aims of the essay and of the novel at this point, Woolf's writings on aesthetics from the thirties profess her desire to bring the two together. Her essays on the visual arts, likewise, draw away from a rigid formalist insistence on the separation of aesthetics from other realms of experience. In 1930, she closes an essay on her sister's paintings by first asserting the formalist separation of the aesthetic sphere "in which mortality does not enter, and psychology is held at bay;" she then, however, reopens the question of art's relationship to morality, which she leaves unanswered: "But is morality to be found there? That was the very question I was asking myself as I came in." In a second essay, drafted four years later but unpublished, Woolf asserted that though her sister represented her subjects as "matter merely: static, statuesque," her art suggests a wide variety of ideas.[31] This theme is repeated in the dialogue published as *Walter Sickert* (1934), in which Woolf compares his painting to prose. While the artists in the conversation adhere to a strictly formalist critique of Sickert's work, Woolf insists on a broader view, making the formalist approach simply one among many. As the artist is praised for his skills as a biographer and storyteller, Woolf concludes that Sickert's strength lies in his hybrid approach: "That is why he draws so many different people to look at his pictures" (*CE* 2:243).

Woolf's decision to make Sickert the subject of Bloomsbury's polyvocal ruminations on art is indicative of the group's increasing anxiety over the desirability of a pure formalism. Through the teens, Sickert had continued his staunchly representational practice, despite Bloomsbury's promotion of abstract painting and formalist theory, remaining publicly skeptical of the group's enthusiasm for Matisse, Picasso, and even the "semi-blighted" Cézanne. Despite this apparent opposition, however, an increasing respect creeps into Bloomsbury's critical assessments of Sickert. As early as 1920, when Fry looked back on his career, one of his regrets was his underestimation of Sickert. In 1921, Clive Bell, insisting Sickert was behind the times, nevertheless compared him to the artists in "remoter parts of Europe" who up until the seventeenth century continued to create "genuine and interesting" gothic art.[32] By Woolf's 1934 essay, the voice of the formalist critic is ready to agree that Sickert "is probably the best painter now living in England" (*CE* 2:244). Bloomsbury's ambivalent relationship to Sickert has been misunderstood, and even misrepresented, by art historians with a greater commitment to the purity of the group's formalism than Fry had himself. By the time Woolf wrote in praise of the "hybrid" Sickert, Fry, in a demonstration of the disdain for critical authority—including his own—that so endeared him to Woolf (*RF* 278, 284, 292, 295–96), was mounting his own since-ignored challenge to the abstract art and pure formalism his theories had done so much to promote. Instead, he too upheld the ideal of "hybrid" painting, in which form and narrative combine to greatest effect.[33]

Woolf's last novel, *Between the Acts* (1941), emerges from this period of turmoil and revision. Like *To the Lighthouse*, it chronicles a woman's struggle for artistic expression, but *Between the Acts* rewrites the staunch formalism of Woolf's earlier text. In contrast to the neat trilateral symmetry of *To the Lighthouse*—and in defiance of the formalist insistence on formal unity as a prerequisite of art's separation from other realms of experience[34]—the formal structure of *Between the Acts* is left radically incomplete, an abruptly truncated triptych with a first "act" of one hundred pages set in the family, then a second (even longer) that is the pageant, followed by an abbreviated return to the situation of the first, which ends almost before it begins. Whereas *To the Lighthouse* concludes with the affirmation of the formalist creative process—Lily's solitary realization of her unique vision, the picture unified about its center line—*Between the Acts* ends with a cooperatively produced pageant, the splintered reflection of a disparate audience, and a gramophone that "gurgled *Unity—Dispersity*. It gurgled *Un .. dis ...* And ceased" (*BA* 201). The formal and authorial disunity is emphasized by Woolf's drastic displacement of the narrative voice in the last paragraphs. Isa reflects on her unhappy marriage as if her life were a text like the pageant ("Surely it was time someone invented a new plot, or that the author came out from the bushes" [*BA* 215]), and the novel ends as she confronts her husband: "the curtain rose. They spoke." Suddenly the pageant, itself comprised of a series of vignettes, has become a play within a larger play, initiating an infinite progression where what seems to be life is always revealed as the art of a larger text. In one move, Woolf violently problematizes the vague formalist fusion of making and finding, violates the assumption of authorial individuality, and shatters all semblance of formal closure.

In its direct engagement with themes of violence—the political violence of war and the sexual violence both of rape and within marriage—*Between the Acts* breaks from the usual restraint of Bloomsbury's artistic and literary production.[35] Woolf's new sense of mission and her impatience with the strict formalism of Bloomsbury's painters emerge in a letter of 1936, where she describes her colleagues as sitting placidly, "looking at pinks and yellows, and when Europe blazes all they do is to screw up their eyes and complain of a temporary glare in the foreground. Unfortunately politics get between one and fiction."[36] Both thematically and formally, *Between the Acts* has less in

common with Bloomsbury aesthetics than it does with Woolf's
description of the generation of writers who matured in the thirties. In
"The Leaning Tower," composed during her work on *Between the Acts*,
Woolf describes how older writers were confined to a limited "box of
toys," "forced to evade the main themes and make do with diversions."
In contrast, books by the thirties authors reveal "a power which, if
literature continues, may prove to be of great value in the future."
"Written under the influence of change, under the threat of war," she
says, the autobiographical novels and poems by the young writers
demonstrate the "courage to tell the truth, the unpleasant truth, about
[themselves]. That is the first step towards telling the truth about other
people." If their work is flawed, Woolf suggests, so be it. The task at
hand is to prepare the way for "the writers of the next generation," who
will not be "a small class of well-to-do young men who have only a
pinch, a thimbleful of experience to give us," but will include women and
others with different stories to tell (*CE* 2:178, 181).[37] The elimination of
anger in favor of the soothing unity of aesthetic closure, which Woolf
herself had upheld in earlier years (*CE* 1:326), now seems a relic of an
earlier, more peaceful age.

In *Between the Acts*, the elderly, well-meaning Lucy Swithin seems
to stand for formalism's foolishly optimistic holism when she is accused
by her juniors of a wishful "one-making" at the expense of a recognition
of suffering:

> She was off, they guessed, on a circular tour of the
> imagination—one-making. Sheep, cows, grass, trees,
> ourselves—all are one. If discordant, producing harmony—if
> not to us, to a gigantic ear attached to a gigantic head. And
> thus—she was smiling benignly—the agony of the particular
> sheep, cow, or human being is necessary; and so—she was
> beaming seraphically ... —we reach the conclusion that *all* is
> harmony, could we hear it .... Well, if the thought gave her
> comfort ... let her think it. (*BA* 175)

This passage could be a parody of the optimism in Clive Bell's *Art*, where
he assured his pre–World War I readers that though "the ideas of men
go buzz and die like gnats," formally significant art lives on in a different
realm "of the God in everything, of the universal in the particular, of the

all-pervading rhythm."[38] With fascism and a second World War threatening everything she held dear, Woolf was with the young in finding no comfort in these platitudes. In "The Leaning Tower," Woolf wonders aloud about what would have happened had she been a rebellious young author of the thirties: "What books I might have written myself?" (*CE* 2:177). *Between the Acts*, in its angry denial of social or aesthetic harmony, begins to answer that question.

Modern feminists, who have been frustrated by what Adrienne Rich describes in Woolf's *Room of One's Own* as "the tone of a woman ... determined not to appear angry, who is *willing* herself to be calm [and] detached," may find satisfaction in recognizing the distance between her strict formalism of the twenties and her writings of the following decade. To see this change as Woolf's complete repudiation of either formalism or its male proponents who were her colleagues in Bloomsbury, however, is to overlook the feminist component in Woolf's initial attraction to formalism, which she saw as an alternative to established aesthetic conventions. It is also to ignore the open-endedness of formalism, in the hands of Roger Fry, as a highly relative, constantly evolving philosophy responsive to changing conditions. If Woolf passed, as my title suggests, through formalism, the voyage did not leave her unmarked. She took from formalism—from Fry in particular—what she admired, and moved on.[39]

Woolf's diary records, on the same day, the completion of "The Leaning Tower" and a breakthrough in her work on *Between the Acts*: "[I] think I've tapped something perhaps—a new combination of the raw & the lyrical." She goes on immediately to tie this accomplishment to her work on Fry's biography: "I think 2 years at Roger may have filled the cistern" (*D* 5:259). If Woolf needed to come to terms with Fry in order to develop her own post-formalist aesthetic, it was not in order to repudiate his influence. On the contrary, telling Fry's story, Woolf seeks to claim his legacy for her project to unite politics and aesthetics. Returning to the question she in 1930 had asked about her sister's painting—"But is morality to be found there?"—Woolf now insists on the extra-aesthetic elements in even Fry's strictest formalist pronouncements. Quoting his remarks on the artist's need to avoid the complacency of stereotype or the easy success of facility, she insists, "morality and conduct, even if they are called by other names, are present; eating and drinking and love-making hum and murmur on the other side of the page" (*RF* 228).

Woolf's post-formalism draws on this belief in the unity of aesthetic and social values. While still refusing the exhortations of Wells, Bennett, and Galsworthy, it engages serious moral issues. And though it rejects a notion of realism constituted as the transmission of authorial (authoritative) knowledge—the detailed catalog of facts Woolf had earlier satirized in Bennett—it renounces as well formalism's attempt to isolate aesthetic experience, suggesting instead the analogous constructedness of art and life. The patterns that emerge from *Between the Acts* are as much social and political as aesthetic, a connection Woolf draws in her biography of Fry when she uses the example of his own life to challenge his claims for aesthetic purity:

> [W]ere they distinct? It seems as if the aesthetic theory were brought to bear upon the problems of private life. Detachment, as he insisted over and over again, is the supreme necessity for the artist. Was it not equally necessary if the private were to continue? That rhythm could only grow and expand if it were detached from the deformation which is possession .... It was difficult to put that teaching into practice. Yet in his private life he had ... forced himself to learn that lesson. (*RF* 214–15)

The model of artistic creativity Lily Briscoe learned in *To the Lighthouse* is here applied explicitly to life, as Woolf transgresses the letter of formalist doctrine in order to broaden the application of its spirit. Is such post-formalism, especially as it is applied to the founder of formalism himself, an anti-formalism that rejects his teaching or an ultra-formalism that seeks to extend its implications beyond the aesthetic realm? To borrow the final words of Fry's *Vision and Design*: "Any attempt I might make to explain this would probably land me in the depths of mysticism. On the edge of that gulf I stop."

NOTES

An earlier version of this article appeared in *Twentieth Century Literature* 38 (Spring 1992): 20–43. Permission to use this material is gratefully acknowledged. My thanks to Patricia Joplin for inspiration, to Carolyn Heilbrun for encouragement, to Diane Gillespie and Brenda Silver for advice, and to Chris Castiglia for all of these, "plus love."

1. See John Hawley Roberts, "Vision and Design in Virginia Woolf," *PMLA* 61 (1946): 835–47; J. K. Johnstone, *The Bloomsbury Group* (New York: Noonday, 1954), 82–91; Allen McLaurin, *Virginia Woolf: The Echoes Enslaved* (Cambridge: Cambridge University Press, 1973); Jonathan R. Quick, "Virginia Woolf, Roger Fry, and Post-Impressionism," *Massachusetts Review* (Winter 1985): 547–70; David Dowling, *Bloomsbury Aesthetics and the Novels of Forster and Woolf* (New York: St. Martin's, 1985).

2. For feminist critiques of American formalism, see Roszika Parker and Griselda Pollock, *Old Mistresses: Women, Art, and Ideology* (New York: Pantheon, 1981), 144–51; and Anne M. Wagner, "Lee Krasner as L.K.," *Representations* 25 (Winter 1989): 42–57. Important works in progress by Ann Gibson, Jonathan Katz, and Kenneth Silver will further fill the need, noted by Wagner, for studies of "the general issues presented by the language of criticism in the 1940's—its sexual stereotypes and expectations" (56).

3. The lingering strength of this attitude is demonstrated in William Feaver "Bloomsbury Painters," *Architectural Digest* 45 (July 1988): 132–37, 182.

4. This list is taken from the definitive early statement of formalism, Fry's "An Essay in Aesthetics," in *Vision and Design* (1920; London: Oxford University Press, 1981), 23–24.

5. Clive Bell, *Art* (1914; New York: Frederick A. Stokes, n.d.), 153; Roger Fry, *The Letters of Roger Fry*, ed. Denys Sutton (London: Chatto and Windus, 1972), 2:369.

6. Dowling, *Bloomsbury Aesthetics*, 104. Here, as in his analyses of other Woolf novels, the relevance of painting is exaggerated by a disconcerting habit of labeling as examples of art the characters' daydreams and mental images.

7. Diane Gillespie points out how Woolf allows this diary entry to reveal more about her ambivalently literary approach to art than does her letter to her sister, the painter Vanessa Bell, describing the same visit to the National Gallery. See "'Oh to be a painter!' Virginia Woolf as Art Critic," *Studies in the Humanities* 10 (June 1983): 28–38.

8. See Frances Spalding, *Roger Fry: Art and Life* (London: Granada, 1980), 211.

9. Quick proposes "largely personal reasons" for Woolf's new fondness for Fry at this time ("Virginia Woolf, Roger Fry, and Post-Impressionism" [552–55, 568]). Without denying their importance, I am tracing the intellectual component of what was both a personal and professional rapprochement.

10. This is the first mention of Fry in the context of art criticism in Woolf's diaries. Hereafter Fry becomes an increasingly prominent and more interesting presence there (*D* 1:134, 140–41, 225). The collected letters of both Fry and Woolf reveal the same burgeoning intimacy.

11. Roger Fry, "An Early Introduction by Roger Fry," in *The Poems of Mallarmé*, ed. Charles Mauron and Julian Bell, trans. Roger Fry (1936; New

York: New Directions, 1951), 295; *Transformations* (London: Chatto and Windus, 1926), 5.

12. Fry, *Letters*, 2:580; Mauron, *The Nature of Beauty in Art and Literature* (London: Hogarth, 1927), 66–67, 71. For Mauron's career in full, see Linda Hutcheon, *Formalism and the Freudian Aesthetic: The Example of Charles Mauron* (Cambridge: Cambridge University Press, 1984).

13. Herbert Marder's *Feminism and Art: A Study of Virginia Woolf* (Chicago: University of Chicago Press, 1968) argues that Woolf did not allow her feminism to contaminate her formalism. Patricia Stubbs's *Women and Fiction* (Brighton: Harvester Press, 1979) charges formalism with constraining Woolf's feminism. Subsequent feminist studies that seek to reconcile Woolf's feminism with her modernism do so by choosing nonformalist definitions of modernism, which are anachronistic to Woolf's stated views; for more detail on this point, see the version of this essay in *Twentieth Century Literature*, 39, n. 8. Perhaps the most disturbing trend in recent feminist treatments of Woolf is the tendency to see her entire involvement with Bloomsbury as incompatible with her feminism; see my "Bloomsbury Bashing," *Genders* 11 (Fall 1991): 58–80.

14. The feminist strategies of Woolf's pieces on Arnold Bennett are outlined (without reference to her formalism) in Beth Rigel Daugherty, "The Whole Contention Between Mr. Bennett and Mrs. Woolf, Revisited," in *Virginia Woolf: Centennial Essays*, ed. Elaine K. Ginsberg and Lana Moss Gottlieb (Troy: Whitson, 1983), 269–94.

15. An interesting connection between Woolf's strategy here and the precedent provided by Bloomsbury's formalist critics is provided by a comparison of her arguments with those in Clive Bell's pacifist pamphlet *Peace at Once* (London: National Labour Press, 1915), which the government seized and burned in 1915. Bell contrasts the abstractions privileged in patriarchal culture—"National Honour," "Civilization," "The Cross," and "Nietzsche"—to the everyday pleasures of "picture palaces and music halls, or sauntering in fine weather through the parks," which might be enjoyed by the young men who were being sent to the front and killed. Bell concludes the latter are more real than—and not worth sacrificing to—the former.

16. Sigmund Freud, "Creative Writers and Day-Dreaming," in *The Standard Edition of the Complete Psychological Works of Sigmund Freud*, ed. James Strachey (London: Hogarth, 1953–1974) 9:143–53. Bell, *Art*, 32.

17. Pioneering and accessible texts include John Berger et al., *Ways of Seeing* (New York: Penguin Books, 1972), 45–64; Linda Nochlin and Thomas B. Hess, eds., *Woman as Sex Object: Studies in Erotic Art 1730–1970* (New York: Arts News Annual, 1972); S. Kent and J. Morreau, *Women's Images of Men* (London: Writers and Readers, 1985), especially Sarah Kent's "Looking Back." Much feminist work on the assumptions of representation and viewing draws heavily on film theory, in particular Laura Mulvey's "Visual Pleasure and Narrative Cinema," *Screen* 16 (Autumn 1975): 6–18.

18. Mauron, *Nature of Beauty*, 58; Roger Fry, "The Artist and Psychoanalysis," in *The New Criticism: An Anthology of Modern Aesthetics and Literary Criticism*, ed. Edwin Berry Burgum (New York: Prentice-Hall, 1930), 193–215, 200–201. On Fry's willingness to insist on this distinction, even to a fellow art historian, see Kenneth Clark's introduction to Roger Fry, *Last Lectures* (London: Macmillan, 1939), xvi–xvii.

19. Bell, *Art*, 15.

20. Erich Auerbach, *Mimesis: The Representation of Reality in Western Literature*, trans. Willard R. Trask (Princeton: Princeton University Press, 1953), 534, 546, 552. My use of Auerbach draws on Patricia Kleindienst Joplin's "The Art of Resistance: Authority and Violence in the Work of Virginia Woolf" (Ph.D. diss., Stanford University, 1984).

21. Macron, *Nature of Beauty*, 24, 76.

22. Joplin, "Art of Resistance," 92.

23. Bell, *Art*, 25.

24. Another token of Fry's influence on *To the Lighthouse* is that Mrs. Ramsay's much-discussed creation, the Boeuf en Daube, was one of his specialities (see Spalding, *Fry*, 128). That the dish was not for Woolf the old family specialty she asserts it was for Mrs. Ramsay (*TTL* 151) is evident from Vanessa Bell's first reaction to the book, which included the inquiry, echoed by many subsequent readers, "But how do you make Boeuf en Daube?" (Vanessa Bell to Virginia Woolf, May 11, 1927, Berg Collection, New York Public Library). An answer is provided in Linda Wolfe's *The Literary Gourmet: Menus from Masterpieces* (New York: Harmony Books, 1989), 234–35.

25. Roger Fry, *Reflections on British Painting* (London: Faber and Faber, 1934), 127. The *finding* versus *making* terminology is drawn from Richard Shiff's critique of Fry in *Cézanne and the End of Impressionism: A Study of the Theory, Technique, and Critical Evaluation of Modern Art* (Chicago: University of Chicago Press, 1984).

26. James Hafley, "Virginia Woolf's Narrators and the Art of 'Life Itself,'" in Virginia Woolf. *Revaluation and Continuity*, ed. Ralph Freedman (Berkeley: University of California Press, 1980), 33.

27. See Bell, *Art*, 8–10.

28. See Simon Watney "The Connoisseur as Gourmet: The Aesthetics of Roger Fry and Clive Bell," in *Formations of Pleasure* (London: Routlege Kegan Paul, 1983). In Greenberg, see, for example, his assertion of the supremacy of "formal culture" over folk art and his equation of popular culture with kitsch in "The Avant-Garde and Kitsch," in *Art and Culture* (Boston: Beacon Press, 1961), 3–21.

29. See Clive Bell, "Criticism: Second Thoughts," in *Since Cézanne* (London: Chatto and Windus, 1923), 162–69. William G. Bywater, Jr., in *Clive Bell's Eye* (Detroit: Wayne State University Press, 1975), argues that such an

acceptance of a diversity of aesthetic responses was always inherent in Bell's theory (77–79).

30. Early formalist essays include Roger Fry, "Art and Life," in *Vision and Design*, 1–15; and Bell, *Art*, 95–105. Outstanding studies of Woolf's social concerns are Carolyn Heilbrun, "Virginia Woolf in her Fifties," in *Virginia Woolf: A Feminist Slant*, ed. Jane Marcus (Lincoln: University of Nebraska Press, 1983), 236–53; Alex Zwerdling, *Virginia Woolf and the Real World* (Berkeley: University of California Press, 1986); and Michele Barrett, introduction to *Virginia Woolf: Women and Writing* (New York: Harcourt Brace Jovanovich, 1979). Woolf, in her biography of Fry, takes pains to explain away his "Art and Life" as a psychological strategy for surviving the war by asserting that great art does not require great cultural conditions (*RF* 214).

31. Virginia Woolf, "Recent Paintings by Vanessa Bell," in *The Bloomsbury Group: A Collection of Memories*, ed. S. P. Rosenbaum (Toronto: University of Toronto Press, 1975), 170–73; "Vanessa Bell's Exhibition," Berg Collection, New York Public Library.

32. Walter Richard Sickert, "Duncan Grant," *Nation and Athenaeum* February 16, 1929, 687; Fry, *Vision and Design*, 288; Bell, *Since Cézanne*, 8.

33. Roger Fry, "The Double Nature of Painting" (1933), *Apollo* 89 (May 1969): 362–71. That this essay was only published in 1969, and then in an abridged version, while the 1920 *Vision and Design*—like Bell's 1914 *Art*—has gone through numerous editions, is indicative of art scholarship's unwillingness to recognize a post-formalist Roger Fry. The most egregious misrepresentation of Fry is Charles Harrison's *English Art and Modernism 1900–1939* (Bloomington: Indiana University Press, 1981).

34. Fry, *Vision and Design*, 31.

35. The thematic violence and formal disunity of *Between the Acts*, though remarkable in their Bloomsbury context, develop tendencies implicit in Woolf's previous novel, *The Years*; see James Naremore, "Nature and History in *The Years*," in Freedman, *Virginia Woolf*, 241–62; and Zwerdling, *Virginia Woolf and the Real World*, 304–5. An excellent analysis of Woolf's authorial strategies in a political context is provided by Patricia Kleindienst Joplin, "The Authority of Illusion: Feminism and Fascism in Virginia Woolf's *Between the Acts*," *South Central Review* 2 (Summer 1989): 88–104. Joplin, however, exaggerates Woolf's distance from the more political members of Bloomsbury, especially Leonard Woolf, whose *Barbarians at the Gate* (London: V. Gollancz, 1939) expresses the attitudes Joplin attributes to Virginia Woolf alone.

36. Virginia Woolf to Julian Bell, June 20, 1936, in Diane Filby Gillespie, *The Sisters' Arts: The Writing and Painting of Virginia Woolf and Vanessa Bell* (Syracuse: Syracuse University Press, 1988), 47.

37. Woolf's argument in "The Leaning Tower" makes more forceful a point she had made in her 1932 "A Letter to a Young Poet," where she admires the violence of contemporary poetry, despite its lack of "beauty" (*CE* 2:182–95). In

"Mr. Bennett and Mrs. Brown" (*CE* 1:326), Woolf earlier derided books that make demands on "life ... in order to complete them."

38. Bell, *Art*, 37, 69.

39. Adrienne Rich, "When We Dead Awaken: Writing as Re-Vision," in *Adrienne Rich's Poetry*, ed. Barbara Charlesworth Gelpi and Albert Gelpi (New York: Norton, 1975), 92. My argument here opposes Jane Marcus, *Art and Anger: Reading Like a Woman* (Columbus: Ohio State University Press, 1988), 73–154.

Chronology

1878   Julia Prinsep Jackson Duckworth (mother to Stella, Gerald and George) marries Leslie Stephen (father of Laura) on March 26.

1879   Vanessa Stephen is born on May 30.

1880   September 8—Julian Thoby Stephen is born; Leonard Woolf is born.

1882   Adeline Virginia Stephen is born at 22 Hyde Park Gate on January 25; Leslie Stephen is made editor of *Dictionary of Literary Biography*.

1883   Adrian Leslie Stephen is born on October 27.

1891   *Hyde Park Gate News* is first produced by the Stephen children.

1895   Julia Stephen dies on May 5; Virginia suffers her first breakdown.

1897   Stella marries Jack Hills; Stella dies on July 19; Virginia attends Greek and history classes at King's College, London.

1899   Thoby Stephen enters Trinity College, Cambridge, and befriends Clive Bell, Saxon Sydney-Turner, Lytton Strachey, and Leonard Woolf.

1900   Vanessa and Virginia attend the May Ball at Cambridge.

1902   Virginia begins Greek lessons with Janet Case; Leslie Stephen is knighted.

1904   Leslie Stephen dies on February 22; Violet Dickinson nurses Virginia during her breakdown; Virginia's first suicide attempt at Dickinson's house; George Duckworth marries; Virginia's first articles are published; move to 46 Gordon Square; Leonard Woolf dines with the Stephens before leaving for Ceylon.

1905   Thoby Stephen initiates "Thursday Evenings" at 46 Gordon Square.

1906   The four siblings go to Greece accompanied by Violet Dickinson; Thoby dies of typhoid on November 20; November 22—Vanessa agrees to marry Clive Bell.

1907   Virginia and Adrian move to 29 Fitzroy Square; reinstate "Thursday Evenings."

1908   Julian Bell is born to Clive and Vanessa in February.

1909   Lytton Strachey proposes marriage; Virginia accepts; they call it off shortly thereafter.

1910   February 10—"The Dreadnought Hoax"; Quentin Bell is born (later Woolf's biographer); November— Opening of first Post-Impressionist Exhibit by Roger Fry at Grafton Galleries; Virginia meets Roger Fry.

1911   July—Leonard Woolf returns from Ceylon, dines at 46 Gordon Square; becomes reacquainted with Virginia; Virginia moves to 38 Brunswick Square with Adrian, Maynard Keynes, Duncan Grant, and (in December) Leonard Woolf; Virginia leases Asheham.

1912   Leonard proposes marriage in January, and is accepted in May after resigning from Colonial Service; Virginia and Leonard Woolf marry in August; they spend their honeymoon in western Europe.

1913   April—*The Voyage Out* taken for publication by Duckworth. Virginia becomes ill in the summer; she tries to commit suicide in September.

1914   Virginia recovers; war is declared; Woolfs move to Richmond.

1915   Woolfs move to Hogarth House, Richmond; February—Virginia is dangerously ill again; *The*

Voyage Out published; Virginia begins to recover in November; starts diary.

1916   Virginia befriends Katherine Mansfield; Vanessa moves to Charleston.

1917   Woolfs start Hogarth Press; they print *Three Jews* and *A Mark on the Wall*.

1918   Armistice is declared; Angelica Bell (daughter of Vanessa and Duncan Grant) is born; Lytton Strachey publishes *Eminent Victorians*.

1919   Duckworth publishes *Night and Day* in October; Hogarth publishes *Kew Gardens* and T.S. Eliot's *Poems*; Woolfs buy Monk's House, Rodmell, after being asked to leave Asheham.

1920   Memoir Club begins.

1921   *Monday or Tuesday* is published in March by Hogarth (as are all subsequent English releases); Virginia is ill through the summer.

1922   *Jacob's Room* is published in October; Virginia meets Vita Sackville-West.

1924   Virginia buys lease to 52 Tavistock Square; they move there in March with the Press; *Mr. Bennet and Mrs. Brown* is published.

1925   *The Common Reader* is published; *Mrs. Dalloway* is published.

1927   *To the Lighthouse* is published.

1928   *Orlando* is published; Virginia receives the *Femina Vie Heureuse* prize; she gives lectures at Girton and Newnham Colleges, which become the genesis for *A Room of One's Own*.

1929   *A Room of One's Own* is published.

1930   She becomes friends with composer Ethel Smyth.

1931   *The Waves* is published; John Lehmann begins at the Press.

1932   Death of Lytton Strachey; *Letter to a Young Poet* is published; *The Common Reader* (second series) is published; Lehmann leaves the Press.

1933   *Flush* is published.

1934   Roger Fry dies; Virginia agrees to write his biography.

1935   *Freshwater* is performed; the strain of writing *The Years* makes Virginia ill.

1936   She is ill most of the year.

1937   *The Years* is published; Julian Bell is killed in the Spanish Civil War.

1938   Lehmann returns to the Press and buys Virginia's half; *Three Guineas* is published; Ottoline Morrell dies.

1939   Move from Tavistock to 37 Mecklenberg Square, with Press; war is declared.

1940   *Roger Fry: A Biography* is published; Mecklenburgh Square is badly damaged in bombing; Hogarth Press moved to Garden City Press in Letchworth.

1941   Virginia commits suicide on March 28; *Between the Acts* is posthumously published.

Works by Virginia Woolf

The Voyage Out, 1915.

The Mark on the Wall, 1917.

Kew Gardens; Night and Day, 1919.

Monday or Tuesday, 1921.

Jacob's Room, 1922.

Mr. Bennett and Mrs. Brown, 1924.

The Common Reader; Mrs. Dalloway, 1925.

To the Lighthouse, 1927.

Orlando, 1928.

A Room's of One's Own, 1929.

On Being Ill, 1930.

The Waves, 1931.

A Letter to a Young Poet; The Common Reader: Second Series, 1932.

Flush: A Biography, 1933.

The Years, 1937.

Three Guineas, 1938.

Reviewing, 1939.

Roger Fry: A Biography, 1940.

Between the Acts, 1941.

"The Death of the Moth" and Other Essays, 1942.

"A Haunted House" and Other Short Stories, 1944.

"The Moment" and Other Essays, 1947.

"The Captain's Death Bed" and Other Essays, 1950.

A Writer's Diary, 1953.

Virginia Woolf and Lytton Strachey: Letters, 1956.

Granite and Rainbow: Essays, 1958.

The Lady in the Lookingglass, 1960.

Contemporary Writers, 1965.

Collected Essays (4 volumes), 1966–1967.

Nurse Lugton's Golden Thimble, 1966.

Mrs. Dalloway's Party, 1973.

Moments of Being, 1976.

Books and Portraits, 1977.

The Letters of Virginia Woolf (Five volumes, edited by Nigel Nicolson and Joanne Trautmann), 1975–1980.

Women and Fiction (edited by Michele Barrett), 1979.

The Diary of Virginia Woolf (edited by Anne Olivier Bell), 1977–1984.

The Letters of Virginia Woolf to Vita Sackville-West, 1984.

The Essays, 1986–1994.

A Passionate Apprentice: The Early Journals, 1897–1909 (ed. by Mitchell Leaska), 1990.

A Woman's Essays, 1992.

The Crowded Dance of Modern Life, 1993.

Works about Virginia Woolf

Abel, Elizabeth. *Virginia Woolf and the Fictions of Psychoanalysis*. Chicago, University of Chicago Press, 1989.

Alexander, Peter F. *Leonard and Virginia Woolf: A Literary Partnership*. Hemel Hempstead, Hertfordshire: Harvester Wheatsheaf, 1992.

Barrett, Eileen, and Patricia Cramer. *Virginia Woolf: Lesbian Readings*. New York: New York University Press, 1997.

Batchelor, John. *Virginia Woolf: The Major Novels*. Cambridge: Cambridge University Press, 1991.

Bell, Clive. *Old Friends: Personal Recollections*. New York: Harcourt, Brace and Company, 1956.

Bell, Quentin. *Virginia Woolf: A Biography* (2 vols). New York: Harcourt, Brace and Company, 1972.

Bell, Vanessa. *Notes on Virginia's Childhood: A Memoir*, ed. R.F. Schaubeck, Jr. New York: Frank Hall, 1974.

Bishop, Edward. *A Virginia Woolf Chronology*. London: Macmillan Press Ltd., 1989.

———. *Macmillan Modern Novelists*. London: Macmillan, 1991.

Bloom, Harold. *Modern Critical Views: Virginia Woolf*. New York: Chelsea House Publishers, 1986.

Caramagno, Thomas C. *The Flight of the Mind: Virginia's Woolf's Art and Manic-Depressive Illness*. Berkeley: University of California Press, 1992.

Chapman, Wayne K., and Janet M. Manson. *Women in the Milieu of Leonard and Virginia Woolf: Peace, Politics, and Education*. New York: Pace University Press, 1998.

Curtis, Vanessa. *Virginia Woolf's Women*. London: Robert Hale, 2002.

da Dilva, N Takei. *Modernism and Virginia Woolf*. Windsor, England: Windsor Publications, 1990.

Darroch, Sandra Jobson. *Ottoline : The Life of Lady Ottoline Morrell*. New York: Coward, McCann & Geoghegan, 1975.

DeSalvo, Louise. *Virginia Woolf's First Voyage: A Novel in the Making*. Totowa, N.J.: Rowman & Littlefield, 1980.

———. *Virginia Woolf: The Impact of Childhood Sexual Abuse on Her Life and Work*. London: The Women's Press, 1989.

Dunn, Jane. *A Very Close Conspiracy: Vanessa Bell and Virginia Woolf*. London: Jonathan Cape, 1990.

Goldman, Jane. *The Feminist Aesthetics of Virginia Woolf: Modernism, Post-Impressionism and the Politics of the Visual*. Cambridge: Cambridge University Press, 1998.

Gordon, Lyndall. *Virginia Woolf: A Writer's Life*. Oxford: Oxford University Press, 1984.

Hussey, Mark, and Vara Neverow. *Virginia Woolf: Emerging Perspectives*. Lanham, Maryland: Pace University Press, 1994.

Kennedy, Richard. *A Boy at the Hogarth Press*. Harmondsworth, Middlesex: Penguin Books, 1978.

Kirkpatrick, B.J. *A Bibliography of Virginia Woolf*. 3rd ed. Oxford: Clarendon Press, 1980.

Laurence, Patricia Ondek. *The Reading of Silence: Virginia Woolf in the English Tradition*. Stanford: Stanford University Press, 1991.

Leaska, Mitchell A. *The Novels of Virginia Woolf: From Beginning to End*. London: Weidenfeld and Nicolson, 1977.

———. *Granite and Rainbow: The Hidden Life of Virginia Woolf*. New York: Farrar, Straus & Giroux, 1998.

———. *Virginia Woolf's Lighthouse: A Study in Critical Method*. London: Hogarth Press, 1970.

Lehmann, John. *Thrown to the Woolfs*. London: Weidenfeld and Nicolson, 1978.

Majumdar, Robin, and Allen McLaurin, eds. *Virginia Woolf: The Critical Heritage*. London: Routledge & Kegan Paul, 1975.

Marcus, Jane, ed. *Virginia Woolf and Bloomsbury: A Centenary Celebration*. London: Macmillan Press, 1987.

Neverow-Turk, Vara, and Mark Hussey, eds. *Virginia Woolf: Themes and Variations*. New York: Pace University Press, 1992.

Nicolson, Nigel. *Portrait of a Marriage*. New York: Atheneum, 1973.

Noble, Joan Russell, ed. *Recollections of Virginia Woolf*. New York: William Morrow, 1972.

Pawlowski, Merry M. *Virginia Woolf and Fascism: Resisting the Dictators' Seduction*. Chippenhame, Wiltshire: Palgrave, 2001.

Peach, Linden. *Virginia Woolf*. Critical Issues Series. New York: St. Martin's Press, 2000.

Poole, Roger. *The Unknown Virginia Woolf*. Cambridge: Cambridge University Press, 1978.

Roe, Sue and Susan Sellars. *The Cambridge Companion to Virginia Woolf*. Cambridge: Cambridge University Press, 2000.

Rose, Phyllis. *Woman of Letters: A Life of Virginia Woolf*. New York: Harcourt Brace Jovanovich, 1978.

Rosenbaum, S.P., ed. *The Bloomsbury Group: A Collection of Memoirs, Commentary and Criticism*. Toronto: University of Toronto Press, 1975.

Rosenberg, Beth Carole, and Jeanne Dubino. *Virginia Woolf and the Essay*. New York: St. Martin's Press, 1998.

Rosenman, Ellen Bayuk. *A Room of One's Own: Women Writers and the Politics of Creativity*. New York: Twayne Publishers, 1995.

Sackville-West, Vita. *The Letters of Vita Sackville-West to Virginia Woolf*. Ed. Louise DeSalvo and Mitchell A. Leaska. London: Virago Press, 1992.

Spalding, Frances. *Roger Fry: Art and Life*. Berkeley: University of California Press, 1980.

———. *Vanessa Bell*. New York: Ticknor & Fields, 1983.

Spater, George, and Ian Parsons. *A Marriage of True Minds*. New York: Harcourt Brace Jovanovich, 1977.

Spilka, Mark. *Virginia Woolf's Quarrel with Grieving*. Lincoln: University of Nebraska Press, 1980.

Stape, J.H., ed. *Virginia Woolf: Interviews and Recollections*. New York: Macmillan, 1995.

Tomlin, Claire. *Katherine Mansfield: A Secret Life*. New York: Knopf, 1988.

Woolf, Leonard. *Beginning Again: An Autobiography of the Years 1911–1918*. New York: Harcourt Brace Jovanovich, 1964.

———. *Downhill All the Way: An Autobiography of the Years 1919–1939*. New York: Harcourt Brace Jovanovich, 1967.

———. *The Journey Not the Arrival Matters: An Autobiography of the Years 1939–1969*. New York: Harcourt Brace Jovanovich, 1964.

———. *Letters of Leonard Woolf*, ed. Frederic Spotts. New York: Harcourt Brace Jovanovich, 1989.

Contributors

HAROLD BLOOM is Sterling Professor of the Humanities at Yale University. He is the author of over 20 books, including *Shelley's Mythmaking* (1959), *The Visionary Company* (1961), *Blake's Apocalypse* (1963), *Yeats* (1970), *A Map of Misreading* (1975), *Kabbalah and Criticism* (1975), *Agon: Toward a Theory of Revisionism* (1982), *The American Religion* (1992), *The Western Canon* (1994), and *Omens of Millennium: The Gnosis of Angels, Dreams, and Resurrection* (1996). *The Anxiety of Influence* (1973) sets forth Professor Bloom's provocative theory of the literary relationships between the great writers and their predecessors. His most recent books include *Shakespeare: The Invention of the Human* (1998), a 1998 National Book Award finalist, *How to Read and Why* (2000), *Genius: A Mosaic of One Hundred Exemplary Creative Minds* (2002), and *Hamlet: Poem Unlimited* (2003). In 1999, Professor Bloom received the prestigious American Academy of Arts and Letters Gold Medal for Criticism, and in 2002 he received the Catalonia International Prize.

CAMILLE YVETTE-WELSH is a Lecturer in English at the Pennsylvania State University. She is also a poet, critic, and freelance writer/editor. Her work has appeared in *Calyx*, *The Women's Review of Books*, *Barrow Street*, and *Foreword Magazine*, among others.

NEIL HEIMS is a freelance writer, editor and researcher. He has a Ph.D. in English from the City University of New York. Neil has also worked on volumes on Albert Camus and J.R.R. Tolkien for Chelsea House.

GEORGE ELLA LYON has been a Writer-in-Residence at Centre College and also taught in the English program there. She is an award-winning author of children's books, and her articles have appeared in *The New York Times Book Review* and the *Journal of Kentucky Studies*.

CHRISTOPHER REED is Associate Professor of Art at Lake Forest College. His books include *Bloomsbury Rooms: Modernism, Subculture, and Domesticity* and the edited critical anthology *A Roger Fry Reader*.

INDEX